W9-CEZ-712

THE BROADVIEW
Introduction to
Literature

*Literary
Non-fiction*

THE BROADVIEW
Introduction to
Literature

Literary Non-fiction

Second Edition

General Editors
Lisa Chalykoff
Neta Gordon
Paul Lumsden

broadview press

BROADVIEW PRESS – www.broadviewpress.com
Peterborough, Ontario, Canada

Founded in 1985, Broadview Press remains a wholly independent publishing house. Broadview's focus is on academic publishing; our titles are accessible to university and college students as well as scholars and general readers. With over 600 titles in print, Broadview has become a leading international publisher in the humanities, with world-wide distribution. Broadview is committed to environmentally responsible publishing and fair business practices.

The interior of this book is printed on 100% recycled paper.

PERMANENT   100%   BIO GAS ENERGY   Ancient Forest Friendly™

Library and Archives Canada Cataloguing in Publication

The Broadview introduction to literature, literary non-fiction / general editors, Lisa Chalykoff, Neta Gordon, Paul Lumsden. — Second edition.

Also published as 1 section in The Broadview introduction to literature.
Includes bibliographical references and index.
ISBN 978-1-55481-406-0 (softcover)

1. Essays. 2. English essays. 3. Creative nonfiction. 4. Creative nonfiction, English. 5. Reportage literature. 6. Reportage literature, English. I. Chalykoff, Lisa, editor II. Gordon, Neta, 1971-, editor III. Lumsden, Paul, 1961-, editor IV. Title: Literary non-fiction. V. Title: Introduction to literature, literary non-fiction.

PN6141.B76 2018   808.84   C2018-901768-6

Broadview Press handles its own distribution in North America:
PO Box 1243, Peterborough, Ontario K9J 7H5, Canada
555 Riverwalk Parkway, Tonawanda, NY 14150, USA
Tel: (705) 743-8990; Fax: (705) 743-8353
email: customerservice@broadviewpress.com

Distribution is handled by Eurospan Group in the UK, Europe, Central Asia, Middle East, Africa, India, Southeast Asia, Central America, South America, and the Caribbean. Distribution is handled by Footprint Books in Australia and New Zealand.

Broadview Press acknowledges the financial support of the Government of Canada through the Canada Book Fund for our publishing activities.

Canada

Interior design and typeset by Eileen Eckert
Cover design by Michel Vrana

PRINTED IN CANADA

Contributors to *The Broadview Introduction to Literature*

MANAGING EDITOR   Marjorie Mather
MANAGING EDITOR, FIRST EDITION   Don LePan
DEVELOPMENTAL AND TEXTUAL EDITOR   Laura Buzzard
EDITORIAL COORDINATOR   Tara Bodie

CONTRIBUTING EDITORS AND TRANSLATORS   Lisa Chalykoff
Neta Gordon
Ian Johnston
David Swain

CONTRIBUTING WRITERS   Laura Buzzard
Andrew Reszitnyk
Paul Johnston Byrne
Tara Bodie

EDITORIAL CONTRIBUTORS

Tara Bodie	Bryanne Manveiler
Alicia Christianson	Amanda Mullen
Joel DeShaye	Virginia Philipson
Victoria Duncan	Anja Pujic
Rose Eckert-Jantzie	David Ross
Emily Farrell	Nora Ruddock
Travis Grant	Kate Sinclair
Karim Lalani	Jack Skeffington
Phil Laven	Helena Snopek
Kellen Loewen	Kaitlyn Till
Melissa MacAulay	Morgan Tunzelmann

PRODUCTION

PRODUCTION COORDINATOR:	Tara Lowes
PROOFREADERS:	Joe Davies
	Judith Earnshaw
	Michel Pharand
DESIGN AND TYPESETTING:	Eileen Eckert
PERMISSIONS COORDINATOR:	Merilee Atos
COVER DESIGN:	Michel Vrana

Contents

Preface

On hearing that Broadview was planning a new anthology designed to provide an overview of literature at the first-year level, more than a few people expressed surprise. What could a new anthology have to offer that really is different—that gives something new and valuable to academics and students alike? We hope that you will find your own answers to that question once you have looked through this volume. Certainly our intent has been to offer something that is in many ways different. We have brought fresh eyes to the process of choosing a table of contents; from Roland Barthes' "The World of Wrestling" to Ivan Coyote's "Tomboys Still," you'll find selections here that have not been widely anthologized elsewhere.

Not everything about *The Broadview Introduction to Literature* is entirely new, of course. Many of the selections will, we hope, be familiar to instructors; as to which of the "old chestnuts" continue to work well in a teaching context, we have in large part been guided by the advice provided to us by academics at a variety of institutions across Canada. But even where familiar authors and selections are concerned, we think you'll find quite a bit here that is different. We have worked hard to pitch both the author introductions and the explanatory notes at a consistent level throughout—and, in both introductions and notes, to give students more by way of background.

For the second edition, we wanted to keep the same balance of fresh and familiar texts while making the anthology as a whole more contemporary and relevant. We have added more literature from the last twenty years, with a particular focus on contemporary Canadian writers; more literature by Indigenous writers; and a work of graphic non-fiction in Scott McCloud's "Understanding Comics."

Finally, you'll find fresh material posted on the companion website associated with the anthology. The site <http://sites.broadviewpress.com/BIL/> features additional material on many literary sub-genres and movements; material on writing essays about literature—and on referencing and citation; a much fuller glossary of literary terms than it is possible to include in these pages; self-test quizzes on the information provided in the introductions to the various genres; and additional selections that we were unable to find space for in the bound book. All are introduced and annotated according to the same principles and presented in the same format as the selections in the bound-book anthology. Those wishing to go beyond these choices may assign any one of the more than 300 volumes in the acclaimed Broadview Editions series, and we can arrange to have that volume bundled together with the bound-book anthology in a shrink-wrapped package, at little or no additional charge to the student.

Any of the genre volumes of the anthology may also be bundled together in special-price shrink-wrapped packages; whatever genres your course covers, and whatever works you would like to cover within those genres, we will do our best to put together a package that will suit your needs. (Instructors should note that, in addition to the main companion website of materials that may be of interest both to students and to instructors, we have posted instructor-related materials on a separate website.)

I do hope you will like what you see—and I hope as well that you will be in touch with any questions or suggestions; we will always be on the lookout for good ideas as to what we should add to the anthology's companion web-site—and/or for what we should look to include in the next edition of *The Broadview Introduction to Literature*.

[D.L., M.M.]

Acknowledgements

The General Editors, managing editors, and all of us at Broadview owe a debt of gratitude to the academics who have offered assistance and feedback at various stages of the project:

Thomas Allen	Alexander Hart
Rhonda Anderson	Ceilidh Hart
Trevor Arkell	Linda Harwood
Veronica Austen	Chandra Hodgson
John Ball	Kathryn Holland
David Bentley	Ashton Howley
Gregory Betts	Renee Hulan
Shashi Bhat	Kathleen James-Cavan
Linda Van Netten Blimke	Karl Jirgens
Nicholas Bradley	Michelle Jordan
Chris Bundock	Diana Frances Lobb
Hilary Clark	Kathryn MacLennan
David Clark	Shelley Mahoney
Jocelyn Coates	Rohan Maitzen
Richard Cole	Laura Manning
Alison Conway	Joanna Mansbridge
David Creelman	Mark McDayter
Heidi J. Tiedemann Darroch	Lindsey McMaster
Carrie Dawson	Susan McNeill-Bindon
Celeste Daphne Derksen	Alexis McQuigge
Joel DeShaye	Craig Melhoff
Lorraine DiCicco	Bob Mills
Kerry Doyle	Stephanie Morley
Monique Dumontet	Maureen Moynagh
Christopher Fanning	Andrew Murray
Sarah Fanning	Russell Perkin
Michelle Faubert	Allan Pero
Triny Finlay	Mike Perschon
Rebecca Gagan	John Pope
Jay Gamble	Phyllis Rozendal
Dana Hansen	Cory Rushton

Laura Schechter

Stephen Schryer

Peter Slade

Marjorie Stone

Marc Thackray

Daniel Tysdal

Molly Wallace

David Watt

Nanci White

David Wilson

Dorothy Woodman

Gena Zuroski-Jenkins

The Study of Literature

The Nobel prize-winning physicist Paul Dirac reportedly said, "The aim of science is to make difficult things understandable in a simple way; the aim of poetry is to state simple things in an incomprehensible way." More recently, noted Language poet Charles Bernstein—whose work typically challenges the limits of simple comprehension—published the poem "Thank you for saying thank you," in which he explicitly takes up the issue of how poetry "states" things:

> This is a totally
> accessible poem.
> There is nothing
> in this poem
> that is in any
> way difficult.
> All the words
> are simple &
> to the point.

Though Bernstein's work is undoubtedly meant to register as ironic, both his poem and Dirac's comment draw attention to the idea that literature uses language in a peculiar way, and that one of the most fundamental questions readers of literature must ask themselves is: "How is this said?" Or—with apologies to Dirac—the question might be: "How do the language choices in this text make a seemingly simple thing—for example, a statement about love, or family, or justice, or grief—not incomprehensible, but rather more than just something simple?"

Another way of approaching the question of how literature works is to consider the way this anthology of literature is organized around the idea of genre, with texts chosen and categorized according to the way they fit into the classifications of poetry, short fiction, drama, and literary non-fiction. One way of organizing an introductory anthology of literature is the historical, in which selections are sorted from oldest to most recent, usually grouped together according to what have become acknowledged as distinctive historical periods of literary output. Another is the topical or thematic, in which historically and generically diverse selections are grouped together according to subject matter, so that students may compare differing attitudes toward, for example, gender relations, personal loss, particular historical events, or the process of growing up. The decision by an editor of an anthology—or the instructor of a course—to select one organizing principle over another is not arbitrary, but reflects a choice in terms of teaching students how to approach the reading of literature. In very simple terms, one might regard the three options thus: the historical configuration emphasizes discovering the "what" and "when" of literature—what is the body of written work that has come to be considered "literature" (especially in terms of tracing the outlines of a national literature), and when were examples from this distinguished corpus written? The thematic configuration emphasizes sorting through the "why" of literature—why do writers turn to literature to work through complex ideas, and what can we make of our complex responses to differing, often competing, stances on various topics? The generic configuration, finally, emphasizes the "how" of literature—how is the text put together? What are its working parts? How does an attention to the formal attributes of a literary piece help the reader understand the way it achieves its intellectual and emotional—its more than just simple—effects?

What do literary critics mean when they refer to genre? The word was introduced into the English language sometime in the late eighteenth century, borrowed from the French word *genre*, which means "kind" or "style" of art, as when the British agricultural reformer Arthur Young refers in his travel narratives to the "genre" of Dutch painting, which he finds wanting in comparison to the work of the Italian masters. We can look back further to the Latin root *genus*, or even the Greek γένος (*génos*), a term which also refers to the idea of a distinct family or clan; thus, the notion of "kind" might helpfully be thought of as a way of thinking about resemblances, relationships, and keys to recognition among the literary genres. Another helpful analogy is the way biologists have taken up the term *genus* as part of the taxonomy of organisms. The term *genus felis*, for example, refers to a particular order of small cats, including such species as the domestic cat (*felis catus*) and the wildcat (*felis silvestris*); both species share common generic attributes, such as a similar size and a preferred diet of small rodents. For biologists and literary critics alike, the concept of genus or genre, respectively, is used to group things together according to a system of shared, identifiable features, with both terms allowing for the idea that larger groupings can be further broken down into even more specific ones (thus we can refer to the various breeds of domestic cats, or the distinctions among the Petrarchan, Shakespearean, and Spenserian sonnets).

Biologists tend to use the word "characteristics" to designate the features of a genus; literary critics, on the other hand, make use of the word "convention," a somewhat more complicated term. Like *characteristics*, the term *conventions* refers to distinguishing elements of a genre, which is why the study of literature requires a thorough understanding of the specialized descriptive vocabulary used to discuss such elements as a text's metre, its narrative point of view, its use of figurative language, etc. The introductions to each section of this anthology will draw attention to this specialized vocabulary, and students will also want to refer to the extensive glossary of literary terms located at the end of the anthology. The idea of convention, though, has additional conceptual importance relating to the way texts are built to be read. While a domestic cat is simply born with retractable claws and a taste for mice, a literary text is constructed, written in a particular way, often with the aim of eliciting a particular response from a reader. The word convention, in this sense, harks back to the legal concept of agreement, so that when writers make use of conventions associated with a genre, they set up a kind of contract with the reader whereby the reader has a sense of what to expect from the text. For example: when the first five minutes of a film include a long shot of the Pentagon, along with a few quickly edited shots of grim-looking military personnel moving quickly through underground hallways, and perhaps a shot of someone in a dark suit yelling into a cellphone, "Operation Silvestris has been aborted!" the audience understands that they are in for some sort of political thriller. They need not know anything about the details of Operation Silvestris to make this interpretive leap, as the presence of a few conventions of the political thriller (the shot of the Pentagon, the phrase "Operation [blank] has been aborted!") are enough to provide the general outline of a contract entered into between film and audience. Likewise, recognizing that a poem has 14 lines and makes use of a rhyming couplet at the end will provide knowledgeable readers of literature with an inkling as to what they should expect, as these readers will be familiar with the structural conventions of the Shakespearean sonnet.

Whereas a legal contract is a fairly straightforward affair—it outlines the terms of agreement for both sides and more or less explicitly refers to the penalties for undermining those terms—the contract between text and reader is multifaceted. One of the most fascinating things about the way writers make use of literary convention is that the terms of agreement are constantly subject to further consideration, thoughtful challenge, or outright derision. Thus, when the speaker of Shakespeare's sonnet 130 refers to his lady's "dun" breasts and "reek[ing]" breath, the point is not to insult his mistress, or even to admire her in a new, more realistic way; rather, the point is to ridicule the way other poets slavishly adhere to the convention that sonnets glorify a woman's beauty, comparing her eyes to the sun and her breath to the smell of roses. This reading is available for the reader who knows that by the time

Shakespeare decided to try his hand at the genre, translations and imitations of the Petrarchan sonnet had been circulating at the Elizabethan court for many decades. Like organisms, or even laws, conventions of literature evolve over time as writers seek to rethink the rules of the form they wish to explore. The speaker in Lillian Allen's "One Poem Town," warns an imaginary writer: "keep it kool! kool! kool! / on the page / 'cause, if yu bring one in / any other way / we'll shoot you with metaphors." Here, Allen—a writer of experimental poetry—both shows and reflects on the way the conventions of genre can create a set of expectations about what constitutes "proper" literature, and how those expectations can be tested.

Is it somehow problematic to inquire too tenaciously into the working parts of a literary text? Does one risk undermining the emotional force of a poem, the sharp wit of a play, or the exciting plot of an adventure tale if one pays too much attention to seemingly mundane issues of plot structure or metre? To paraphrase a common grievance of the distressed student: by examining the way literature works, are we, somehow, just wrecking it? These questions might, paradoxically, recall Dirac's complaint that literature makes simple things incomprehensible: while we know that literature can manage to communicate difficult notions, making what is mysterious more comprehensible, it is often difficult to articulate or make a viable argument about how it does so. By paying attention to the way a text is built and to the way an author constructs his or her end of the contract, the reader can begin to understand and respond explicitly to the question of how literature produces its particular effects.

Consider the following two textual excerpts:

> Come live with me and be my love,
> And we will all the pleasures prove.
> (Christopher Marlowe, 1590)

> Boom, boom, boom, let's go back to my room,
> And we can do it all night, and you can make me feel right.
> (Paul Lekakis, 1987)

Based on a quick reading, which excerpt is more appropriate for inclusion in a Valentine's Day card? A poll of employees at Hallmark, not to mention the millions of folks invested in the idea that Valentine's Day is a celebration of romance, would likely make an overwhelming case for the Marlowe excerpt. But why? Answering that question might involve a methodological inquiry into how each excerpt produces a particular response, one which might be broken down into five stages:

Level One: Evaluation—Do I like this text? What is my gut reaction to it? No doubt, most students of literature have heard an instructor proclaim, with more or less vitriol, "It doesn't matter if you like the poem/story/play! This is a literature class, not a book club!" And, while it is true that the evaluative response does not constitute an adequate final critical response to a text, it's important to acknowledge one's first reaction. After all, the point of literature is to produce an effect, sometimes an extreme response. When a text seems confusing, or hilarious, or provocative, or thrilling, it prompts questions: How are such effects produced using mere words in particular combinations? Why would an author want to generate feelings of confusion, hilarity, provocation, etc.? How am I—the reader—being positioned on the other end of such effects?

Level Two: Interpretation—What is the text about? This is a trickier level of reading than it might seem. Students sometimes think, mistakenly, that all literature—and especially poetry—is "open to interpretation," and that all interpretations are therefore correct. This line of thinking leads to snap, top-down interpretations, in which the general "mood" of the text is felt at a gut level (see above), and the ensuing reading of the poem is wrangled into shape to match that feeling. It is sometimes helpful to think about interpretation as a kind of translation, as in the way those who work at the United Nations translating talking points from Arabic to Russian are called "interpreters." Though no translation is flawless, the goal of simultaneous translation is to get as close as possible to the meaning of the original. Thus, an interpretation should be thought of as a carefully paraphrased summary or, for particularly dense works, a line by line explication of the literary text, both of which may require several rereadings and some meticulous use of a dictionary. As with reading for evaluation, reading for interpretation can help generate useful critical questions, such as: How does the way this text is written affect my attitude toward the subject matter? What is the point of all the fancy language, which makes this text more or less difficult to interpret? Now that I've figured out what this text is about—at least in terms of its subject matter—can I begin to determine what sorts of themes are being tackled?

A note about the distinction between subject matter and **theme**: while these terms are sometimes used interchangeably, the notion of theme differs from subject matter in that it implies an idea about or attitude toward the subject matter. A good rule of thumb to remember is that theme can never be summed up in just one word (so, there is no such thing as the theme of "Love" or "Family" or "Women"). Whereas the subject matter of Shakespeare's sonnet "Shall I compare thee to a summer's day" is admiration or the nature of beauty, one theme of the poem, arguably, is that the beloved's good qualities are best made apparent in poetry, and that art is superior to nature. Another theme of the poem, arguably, is that the admiration of youth is best accomplished by someone older. Thus, identifying a text's subject matter via interpretation aims to pinpoint a general topic, while the process of contemplating a text's theme is open to elaboration and argumentation.

Level Three: Description—What does the text look like, at least at first glance? Can you give a quick account of its basic formal features? At this level of reading, one starts to think about how a text is built, especially in terms of basic generic features. For example, are we dealing with poetry? Short fiction? Drama? If poetry, can we identify a sub-genre the text fits into—for instance, the sonnet, the ode, or the elegy—and can we begin to assess whether the author is following or challenging conventions associated with that genre? Of course, answering these questions requires prior knowledge of what, for example, a conventional ode is supposed to look like, which is why the student of literature must have a thorough understanding of the specific terminology associated with the discipline. At this level of reading, one might also begin to think about and do some preliminary research on when and where the text was written, so that the issues of literary history and cultural context are broached; likewise, one might begin to think about who is writing the poem, as the matter of the author's societal position might prove a fruitful avenue for further investigation. Thus, a consequent objective at this level of reading is to map the terrain of inquiry, establishing some general facts about the text as building blocks that underpin critical analysis.

Level Four: Analysis—How are particular formal features working, especially as they interact with content? The word analysis comes from the Greek terms ἀνά- (ana-), meaning "throughout," and λύειν (lysis), meaning "to loose." Thus, the procedure for analysis involves taking a text and shaking it apart in order to see more clearly all its particular bits and pieces. This level of reading is akin to putting a text under a microscope. First, one has to identify individual formal features of the text. Then one needs to consider how all the parts fit together. It is at this level that one's knowledge of generic conventions and particular literary techniques—the way figurative language works, the ways in which rhythm and rhyme affect our response to language, the way plotting and point of view can be handled, and so on—is crucial. It may be the case that not everything one notices will find its way into an essay. But the goal at this level of reading should be to notice as much as possible (and it is usually when working at this level that an instructor will be accused of "reading too much into a text," as if that image of a moth beating its wings against a window means nothing more than that the moth is trapped, and that it just happens to have been included in a work). Careful analysis shows that nothing in a text "just happens" to be there. A text is constructed out of special uses of language that beg to be "read into." Reading at this level takes time and a certain amount of expertise so as to tease out how the work is built and begin to understand the connections between form and content.

Level Five: Critical Analysis—How do the formal elements of a literary work connect with what the work has to say to the reader? It is at this level of reading that one begins to make an argument, to develop a thesis. In order to construct a viable thesis, one needs to answer a question, perhaps one of the questions that arose at an earlier level of reading. For example, why does this poem, which seems on the surface to be about love, make use of so many images that have to do with science? What is up with this narrator, who seems to be addressing another character without in any way identifying who he is speaking to? What is significant about the fact that the climax of this play hangs on the matter of whether a guy is willing to sell a portrait? It is at this level of reading, rather than at the level of interpretation, that the literary critic is able to flex his or her creative muscles, as a text poses any number of viable questions and suggests any number of viable arguments. Note, however, that the key word here is "viable." In order to make an argument—in order to convincingly answer a question posed—one must have the textual evidence to make the case, evidence that has been gleaned through careful, meticulous, and thoughtful reading.

Returning now to the two texts, let's see if we can come up with one viable argument as to why Marlowe's text seems more likely to show up in a Valentine's Day card, going through each level of reading to build the foundation—the case—for making that argument.

Level One: Evaluation. At first glance, the Marlowe text just seems more romantic than the Lekakis text: it uses flowery words and has a nice flow to it, while the phrase "do it all night" is kind of blunt and unromantic. On a gut level, one might feel that a Valentine's Day card should avoid such blunt language (although this gut reaction might suggest a first useful research question: why should romance be associated with flowery language rather than blunt expressions?).

Moving on to **Level Two: Interpretation.** Well, the Lekakis text is certainly the more straightforward one when it comes to interpretation, though one has to know that the phrase "do it" refers to having sex as opposed to some other activity (and it is interesting to note that even in the more straightforward text, the author has used a common euphemism). The phrase "Boom boom boom" seems to be untranslatable, which begs the question of why the author used it. Is the phrase still meaningful, even if it's just a series of sounds?

As for the Marlowe text, a careful paraphrase would go something like this: "Move in with me and be my lover, and we can enjoy all kinds of pleasures together." Hmmm—wait a minute: what does the author mean by "pleasures"? Eating good food? Playing card games? Though the word is arguably vague, the references in the first line to moving in together and love make it pretty clear that "pleasures" is another euphemism for having sex (though perhaps a more elegant one than "doing it").

If both texts can be interpreted similarly—both are the words of a would-be lover trying to convince the object of his/her affection to have sex—why does it matter which phrase ends up in a Valentine's Day card? What are the significant differences between each text that cause them to generate distinct gut responses?

Level Three: Description. The Marlowe text, at least this piece of it, is a **couplet**, written in iambic **tetrameter** (or eight syllables in each line that follow the rhythmic pattern of unstressed/stressed). The language is flowery, or, to use a slightly more technical phrase, the **diction** is elevated, which means that this is not the way people normally talk in everyday life. In fact, there seems to have been a lot of attention paid to making the words sound pleasing to the ear, through patterns of rhythm and rhyme, and also through patterns of alliteration in the consonants (of the soft "l" sound in the first line, and then of powerful plosives at the end of the second).

The Lekakis text also makes use of rhyme, but in a different way: each line includes an **internal rhyme**, so that "boom" rhymes with "room" and "night" rhymes with "right." The rhythmic pattern is harder to make sense of, as there is a different number of syllables in each line and a lot of short, sharp words that undermine a sing-song effect. The sound effects of the text are comparatively harsher than in the Marlowe text, with many "b" and "k" and "t" sounds.

The Marlowe text was written in the 1590s, while the Lekakis text is a popular dance song from the 1980s; it might be interesting to follow up on the distinct cultural contexts out of which each work emerges. It might also be interesting to examine how each text thematizes the subject of having sex: whereas the Marlowe text seems to promote the attitude that the "pleasures" of sex should be tried out (to "prove" in sixteenth-century English meant to test or to try out) within the context of "living with" someone, or that love and sex go hand-in-hand, the Lekakis text seems to suggest that even sex on one "night" in someone's "room" can make one feel "right." Or, good sex has nothing at all to do with love.

Because these texts are so short and are fairly simple, much of the work of **Level Four: Analysis** has already been touched on. A closer inspection of the use of rhyme and **alliteration** in the Marlowe text demonstrates the way the poem insists on the idea that love can be "proved" by sex, while the internal rhyming of the words "me," "be," and "we" further indicates a strong emphasis on how the joining of two people represents a significant change. The use of elevated diction is consistent, suggesting that discussions of love and sex are worthy of serious consideration.

As for the Lekakis text, a major point to analyze is the phrase "Boom boom boom." Is this **onomatopoeia**? If so, what "sense" is the sound trying to express? The sound of sex? If so, what kind of sex are we talking about here? Or is it the sound of something else, perhaps dancing (as is suggested by the cultural context out of which the text emerges)? Maybe the phrase is simply meant to express excitement? What do we make of the plain speech the text employs? Does the use of such diction debase notions of sex, or is it simply more candid about the way sex and love might be separated?

As you can see, the level of **Critical Analysis**, or argument, is quickly and organically developing. If the research question one decides on is, What is interesting about the distinct way each text thematizes the relationship between love and sex?, a viable argument, based on evidence gleaned from close reading, might be: "Whereas Marlowe's text suggests that the pleasures of sex are best discovered within the context of a stable, long-term relationship, the text by Lekakis asserts that sex can be enjoyed in and of itself, undermining the importance of the long-term relationship." One might take this argument further. Why is what you have noted significant or particularly interesting? A possible answer to that question—and an even more sophisticated thesis—might be: "Thus, while the Lekakis text is, on the surface, less romantic, its attitude toward sex is much less confining than the attitude presented in Marlowe's text." Or, one might pursue an entirely different argument: "Whereas Marlowe's text indicates that sex is to be enjoyed mutually by two people, the Lekakis text implies that sex is something one 'does' to another person. Further, it implies that sex is a fairly meaningless and potentially aggressive activity."

The above description of the steps taken toward critical analysis shows how students of literature are meant to approach the works they read. What the description does not convey is why one would bother to make the effort at all, or why the process of critical literary analysis is thought to be a meaningful activity. In order to answer that question, it is helpful to consider how the discipline of literary studies came to be considered a worthwhile course of study for university and college students.

The history of literary studies is both very old and, in terms of the study of English literature, very fresh. In the fifth century, Martianus Capella wrote the allegory *De nuptiis Philologiae et Mercurii* ("The Marriage of Philology and Mercury"), in which he described the seven pillars of learning: grammar, dialectic, rhetoric, geometry, arithmetic, astronomy, and musical harmony. Collectively, such subjects came to be referred to as the liberal arts; as such, they were taken up by many of the high medieval universities as constituting the core curriculum. During the Early Modern period, the study of the so-called *trivium* (grammar, dialectic, rhetoric) was transformed to include the critical analysis of classical texts, i.e., the study of literature. As universities throughout Europe, and later in North America, proliferated and flourished between the sixteenth and nineteenth centuries, the focus remained on classical texts. As Gerald Graff explains, "In theory, the study of Greek and Latin was supposed to inspire the student with the nobility of his cultural heritage." (Somewhat paradoxically, classical texts were studied primarily in terms of their language use as opposed to their literary quality, perhaps because no one read or spoke Greek or Latin outside the classroom.) Until the late nineteenth century, the university system did not consider literary works written in English (or French or German or Italian) to be worthy of rigorous study, but only of *appreciation*. As Terry Eagleton notes in *Literary Theory: An Introduction*, the reading of works of English Literature was thought best left to working-class men, who might attend book clubs or public lectures, and to women; it was "a convenient sort of non-subject to palm off on the ladies, who were in any case excluded from science and the professions." It was only in the early twentieth century—hundreds of years after the founding of the great European universities—that literature came to be taken seriously as a university or college subject.

Over the past century and more, the discipline of literary studies has undergone a number of shifts. In the very early twentieth century, literature was studied largely for the way in which it embodied cultural tradition; one would learn something about being American or British by reading so-called great works of literature. (As British subjects, Canadians were also taught what it was to be a part of the British tradition.) By mid-century the focus had shifted to the aesthetic properties of the work itself. This fresh approach was known as Formalism and/or the New Criticism. Its proponents advocated paying close attention to literary form—in some cases, for an almost scientific approach to close reading. They tended to de-emphasize authorial biography and literary history. The influence of this approach continues to be felt in university and college classrooms (giving rise to such things as, for example, courses organized around the concept of literary genre). But it is important to keep in mind here that the emphasis on form—on generic conventions, on literary terminology, on the aesthetic as opposed to the cultural, philosophical, or moral qualities of literature—is not the only way to approach the study of literature, but was, rather, institutionalized as the best, most scholarly way. The work of close reading and producing literary criticism is not in any way "natural," but is how the study of literature has been "disciplined"; thus the student in a literature classroom should not feel discouraged if the initial steps of learning what it is he or she is supposed to be doing are challenging or seem strange.

The most recent important shift to have occurred in the "disciplining" of literary studies was the rise in the 1960s and 1970s of what became known as "literary theory." There is not room enough here to adequately elucidate the range of theories that have been introduced into literary studies, but a crude comparison between how emerging methods were set in opposition to New Criticism (which is itself a type of literary theory) may be useful. John Crowe Ransom's *The World's Body*—a sort of manifesto for New Criticism—argues that the work of the literary critic must strenuously avoid, among other things, "Any other special studies which deal with some abstract or prose content taken out of the work ... [such as] Chaucer's command of medieval sciences ... [or] Shakespeare's understanding of the law." In other words, the New Critic should focus solely on the text itself. In contrast, those today who make use of such theoretical frameworks as New Historicism, Gender Studies, or Postcolonial Studies will strenuously *embrace* all manner of "special studies" in order to consider how the text interacts with context. As Anne Stevens points out in *Literary Theory and Criticism*, "A cornerstone of literary theory is a belief in the cultural construction of knowledge . . . literary theory gives you a way to step back and think about the constructedness of culture and reflect upon your own preconceptions." For the student of literature trying to work out how to answer the question: "Why is what I have noticed in the text significant?", literary theory provides an extensive set of vocabularies and methodologies. For example: a New Historicist or a Marxist approach might help a student inquire into how a particular poem illuminates historical notions of class divisions. A Gender Studies approach might be useful for an examination of what a particular play can tell us about changing conceptions of masculinity. A Semiotic approach might consider the complex set of meaning systems gestured toward in the image of a police uniform described in a science fiction story. And, though it might seem that the focus on form that so defines the New Critical approach becomes irrelevant once Literary Theory arrives on the disciplinary scene, the fact is that most field practitioners (i.e., writers of literary criticism) still depend heavily on the tools of close reading; formal analysis becomes the foundation on which a more theoretical analysis is built.

Thus, we might consider a sixth level of reading: advanced critical analysis. At this level the stakes are raised as arguments about why a text's formal construction is meaningful are set within a larger conceptual framework. The work of advanced critical analysis requires that the literary critic think about and research whatever conceptual framework is being pursued. For example, after noticing that the Marlowe text and the Lekakis text are written about 400 years apart, one might further research cultural attitudes toward sex in the two time periods to come up with another, even more sophisticated, layer of argumentation, one which would not only provide insight into two literary texts, but show how the comparative analysis of such texts tells us something about how viewpoints on sex have shifted. Or, after noticing that both texts are written by male authors, one might further research and consider what they reveal about masculine approaches to sex and seduction. Or, after discovering that Marlowe's poem follows the conventions of **pastoral** poetry, or that "Boom boom boom, let's go back to my room" became popular within the LGBT community, one might contemplate and develop an argument about the implications of the way sex is idealized and/or becomes part of a complex cultural fantasy. Or, after discovering that Marlowe presented homoerotic material frequently in his other writing (in his poem "Hero and Leander," for example, he writes of one of the male protagonists that "in his looks were all that men desire"), one might inquire into the ways in which the author's or narrator's sexual orientation may or may not be relevant to a discussion of a love poem. To put it bluntly (and anachronistically), does it matter if Marlowe was gay?

Because the reading of literature entails a painstaking, thoughtful interaction with some of the most multifaceted, evocative, and provocative uses of language humans have produced, thinking about such work critically may tell us something about what it means to be human.

[N.G.]

Literary Non-Fiction

Literary non-fiction is a diverse genre with a long history—yet its nature is hard to pin down. A work of literary non-fiction is nowadays almost always written in prose, but it may be an essay, a memoir, or a piece of journalism. It may be written for any one of a wide range of purposes. It may be as short as a page or two, or it may be of book length.

No work that calls itself "non-fiction" can be the product of pure invention—if you make up the story, you are writing fiction. Yet the line that separates fiction from non-fiction may sometimes be hard to determine. Many authors of literary non-fiction consider it a legitimate practice to shape the presentation of events or characters in an essay or a memoir in ways that deviate from the specifics of what actually happened. George Orwell, one of the most highly acclaimed writers of literary non-fiction of the twentieth century, is known to have done this frequently. So too does Barack Obama, who, in the preface to *Dreams from My Father*, candidly acknowledges that at least part of what he has written is, in some sense, fiction:

> Although much of this book is based on contemporaneous journals or the oral histories of my family, the dialogue is necessarily an approximation of what was actually said or relayed to me. For the sake of compression, some of the characters that appear are composites of people I've known, and some events appear out of precise chronology.

In other words, the writer has felt at liberty to sift and shape the material to give a personal view of what seems to him to be, in his words, "some granite slab of truth." Critics may reach different conclusions as to whether or not the picture that emerges in such writing does in fact present "some granite slab of truth," but what is equally necessary in this genre is that the writing itself is worthy of critical attention—that it be thought of as literature.

Literary Non-Fiction and Academic Non-Fiction

The form that literary non-fiction most frequently takes is that of the essay. But an *essay* in this sense is something very different from the kind of essay that university students are asked to read (and, usually, to write) when they take courses in academic subjects. For the most part, students are taught that an academic essay should be distanced and impersonal. It should be structured according to established conventions of its academic discipline. And according to these conventions, the academic essay should strive for objectivity; subjective reflections have little place in this kind of writing. The task of the essay writer is not to sway the reader through description or narration or emotional appeal of any sort, but rather to analyze evidence in support of an argument. Whether that argument is made inductively or deductively, an academic essay should display careful reasoning. It should also cite references to support its argument—and to enable others to verify the evidence and use it in their own scholarship.

The sort of essay that constitutes a work of literary non-fiction is none of these things. Though it may sometimes marshal evidence in support of a reasoned argument, it may also employ narration and description and emotional appeal. It may be loosely structured. It is more likely to be personal in tone. And it will normally not include any cited sources. Whereas the academic essay is generally addressed to an audience within a particular scholarly academic discipline, literary non-fiction is typically addressed to a broad audience. It aims to interest and entice readers and to give them pleasure, in the way that literature gives pleasure—through the use of well-crafted images, figurative language, and symbols, by ordering events to create suspense, and by creating interesting non-fictional "characters" to engage us.

Such pleasure is not contingent on the writer's topic being pleasurable. Just as a novel about horrific events can be, *as literature*, enjoyable as well as interesting to read, so too a piece of literary non-fiction about horrific events can be, *as literature*, enjoyable. Conveying in memorable and affecting ways the "unspeakable" is an important function of literature. Philip Gourevitch's piece in this volume, reflecting on the nature of genocide and on having seen the aftermath of a massacre, falls squarely into this category. But if, as a general question, we ask what sorts of topics literary non-fiction addresses, there is no simple answer. The writer may work through any one of a wide range of structures in trying to mediate a reader's understanding of an endless variety of topics. Examples in this volume include an exploration of a father's life (Miriam Toews's memoir); an argument about the appeal of wrestling (Roland Barthes); an exploration of why sports memoirs are terrible (David Foster Wallace); and an exploration of what it means to have brown skin in a world that values whiteness (Kamal Al-Solaylee).

History of the Genre

Given that literary non-fiction has only recently begun to receive considerable attention as a distinct literary genre, one might easily imagine that writing of this sort would be a relatively recent phenomenon. In fact, its roots go almost as far back as do those of poetry and drama. Like them, the genre of literary non-fiction has strong roots in the classical cultures of ancient Greece and Rome. The ancients referred to the process of communication as *rhetoric*. Broadly defined, rhetoric may be said to be involved in almost anything to do with the study of cultural messages, with any communication that attempts to persuade, with almost every human effort to express thoughts coherently so as to communicate them to others. In practice, the Greeks and Romans defined rhetoric much more narrowly. Classical rhetoric was an art whose precepts were designed to help orators (*rhetors*) organize and deliver their arguments in a methodical, articulate, and persuasive way. That may sound a long way from the literary non-fiction of today—may sound, indeed, of more relevance to the roots of the modern academic essay than to those of literary non-fiction. And there can be no question of the relevance of classical rhetoric to the history of academic argument. But historians suggest that the modern essay as a work of literary non-fiction may also be found in embryonic form in the works of some classical writers—not least of all in a work now almost two thousand years old, the *Moral Letters* of the Roman Stoic philosopher Lucius Annaeus Seneca (usually known simply as Seneca).

Though the 124 pieces that make up the *Moral Letters* are written as letters to the then-governor of Sicily, Lucilius—each one begins "Seneca greets his Lucilius"—in every other respect the epistles far more closely resemble what we now call literary non-fiction than they do modern-day personal letters. They are personal in tone, to be sure, but they include little or nothing relating to the particulars of the personal relationship between Seneca and Lucilius. They seem rather to address a general audience. They sometimes try to persuade, and at others, offer rich description (as when Seneca gives us a picture of the dining table or describes the master whose greed has filled his distended belly). They as often appeal to the senses and to the emotions as to reason. And the topics tend to be broad and range widely, from drunkenness to scientific invention, to how a love of sports can become excessive, to the issue of equality between men and women. Seneca is thought of today primarily as a philosopher, but in the Moral Letters his writing is far closer to that of today's writer of literary essays than it is to the writing of most contemporary philosophers.

In the post-medieval era the literary essay is generally said to have begun with the sixteenth-century French writer Michel de Montaigne, known in his day as the "French Seneca." Like Seneca, Montaigne wrote short pieces on a wide variety of broad topics ranging from marriage to study, education, and various aspects of current affairs. But Montaigne's pieces tend to be both more closely reasoned than those of Seneca, and looser in structure. More often than not they explore an idea rather than set out an argument in favour of a predetermined position. Montaigne saw writing of this sort less as a means of persuading the reader to accept a certain conclusion than as a means of trying to grope one's way toward understanding. Hence the name he gave to these short pieces—*essais*, or, in English, *attempts* or *tries*. (The connection is a direct one; among its definitions of *essay* the *Oxford English Dictionary* offers the following: "the action or process of trying or testing.") And always, while attempting to understand some aspect of an idea or of the world, Montaigne was attempting to understand himself—reflecting on his own thoughts, impulses, and desires. In the preface to the *Essais* Montaigne famously declares, "lecteur, je suis moi-même la matière de mon livre" ("reader, I am myself the subject of my book"). In all these respects—the looseness of structure, the vision of writing as a means of groping toward understanding, the tendency to use the essay to explore the outside world and the self simultaneously—Montaigne's writing continues to exert an influence on literary non-fiction.

The history of the literary essay in English is extraordinarily varied. It is often said to begin in early seventeenth-century England with the essays of Francis Bacon. With the eighteenth century came the pointed political and literary essays of Samuel Johnson and Jonathan Swift, and the beginnings of literary journalism. The nineteenth century brought the cultural criticism of Charles Dickens, Matthew Arnold, and George Eliot in Britain, and the personal-philosophic essays of Henry David Thoreau and Ralph Waldo Emerson in the United States. In the twentieth century the range of literary non-fiction became broader still, from Virginia Woolf's essays on gender and society and George Orwell's explorations of politics and culture, to the fresh approaches to form and the tremendous variety of subject matter that characterize the literary non-fiction of late twentieth- and early twenty-first-century writers from every corner of the globe. Across this diversity, though, direct links to the traditions of Montaigne and Seneca remain—in tone, style, structure, and rhetorical strategies.

Style and Structure, Argument, and Rhetoric

Let's return to our comparison of how arguments are presented in the modern academic essay versus literary non-fiction. As we have said, reason and logic are central to what the writer of the academic essay strives for, and the logic of the argument is made overt through such conventions as thesis statements and topic sentences. Anything that might impede an impersonal and objective presentation of a reasoned argument is often said to be inappropriate in an academic essay. Rhetorical flourishes are kept to a minimum. The structure in which an argument is presented tends to be standardized. The pronoun "I" is often said to have no place here, and the same is said of personal details or reflections. Style and structure, in short, are conventionalized in order for the writer to be as unobtrusive as possible—and in order to allow reasoned argument to shine through.

In literary non-fiction, on the other hand, a range of structures is available to the writer, and the adoption of a personal tone and a unique style are often very much a part of the presentation of the "argument." Why is the word "argument" put in quotation marks here? To make clear that, in the context of literary non-fiction, *argument* is not to be taken in the same sense as it is with most academic non-fiction. The argument of a piece of literary non-fiction is the line along which ideas are connected; it may be much looser and less overt than the argument of the typical academic paper of today, and its logic may be implicit, to be sought out by the reader.

Whether we are looking at non-literary academic arguments or those of literary non-fiction, the vocabulary of classical rhetoric remains highly useful when it comes to naming the elements of argument. According to one of the most influential classical rhetorical manuals, *Rhetorica ad Herennium* (which dates from the first century BCE), rhetoric has five canons or general, fundamental principles: invention, arrangement, style, memory, and delivery. As may readily be inferred from the last two items on that list, the expectation was that rhetorical arguments would be delivered orally through a speech (by a *rhetor*) rather than in writing. But the strength and originality of the ideas (invention), the way in which they are arranged, and the style with which they are presented are concepts that remain relevant to non-fiction writing of all sorts.

The *Rhetorica ad Herennium* also sets out guidelines for the layout of an argument (in classical terminology, its *disposition*), specifying that it should include the following elements:

- exordium (introduces the argument)

- narration (states the issue; may supply background or explore the history of the issue)

- division (separates and lists the parts under discussion)

- confirmation (elaborates and supports the *rhetor*'s position)

- confutation (refutes opposing arguments)

- peroration (conclusion)

We may observe these elements in Seneca's writing (see sites.broadviewpress. com/BIL)—how he separates the parts under discussion, how he anticipates (and refutes) the arguments of his opponents. Aside perhaps from *exordium* and *peroration*, though, it may well be thought that such concepts are of limited use in analyzing the contemporary literary essay. But from time to time they may indeed be useful in discussing academic non-fiction. We may see traces of the classical rhetorical strategies of narration and division, for example, in the way in which David Foster Wallace makes his case for why reading a sports memoir is inevitably a disappointment, despite (or perhaps because of) the physical genius of athletes.

Ancient guides to rhetoric also often considered arguments as belonging to one of three types: deliberative (concerned with the future), judicial (sometimes referred to as forensic; concerned with the past), and epideictic (celebratory arguments). These classifications too may sometimes be helpful in discussions of literary non-fiction. When Mark Twain addresses an imaginary audience in "Advice to Youth," he creates an epideictic argument. Roland Barthes, as he explores "The World of Wrestling," makes a judicial or forensic argument (as do several of the other selections). Deliberative arguments in anything close to a pure form, however, are rarely found in literary non-fiction; they occur far more frequently in politicians' speeches, in the arguments of newspaper and television commentators—or in the world of advertising.

Perhaps of greater relevance to today's literary non-fiction are the three categories of appeal that are set out in classical rhetoric (from the early Greek philosopher Aristotle on down): *logos*, *pathos*, and *ethos*. All three are widely and usefully employed in many discussions of literary writing today.

Logos is often translated as *logic*, and to a large extent appeals based on *logos* may indeed be appeals that are logical in nature. But in the world of rhetoric such appeals are not always made according to the principles of inductive or deductive logic that apply to most academic essays. The meaning of *logos* in the ancient world was multi-faceted; it could mean *reason* or *logic*, but it could also simply mean *word*; in the context of literary non-fiction, an appeal based on *logos* may perhaps best be understood as an appeal based on the ideas that the words hold. The rational arguments that Seneca makes—appealing to the principle of fairness and citing the benefits of treating one's slaves or servants well—represent appeals to *logos*. Much the same can be said of Barthes's arguments about the moral content of wrestling. These are arguments that in large part make appeals to *logos* based on traditional principles of logical reasoning. But Miriam Toews also makes an appeal to *logos* when she recounts the history in the Mennonite church of shunning those "out of faith"—a category that included those suffering from depression or despair—and then writes that she "can't help thinking" that this history of shunning had "just a little to do with" the ways in which her father tried to deal with his depression. Toews's line of reasoning cannot be said to follow the same sorts of logical steps that the arguments of Barthes do—and she makes no claims to have reached an airtight conclusion. Yet her appeal to *logos* may be more powerful than that of any of the other pieces included here. Rather than establishing the tenets of and the conclusion to an argument, her appeal to *logos* suggests connections. And rather than demonstrating irrefutably that those connections exist, she persuades us that they are likely to have played a real part in what happened to her father. Giving readers freedom in this way to discern an argument's logic by forging connections for themselves is one important way in which the genre of literary non-fiction may exert powerful effects.

The word *pathos* is sometimes thought to hold pejorative connotations, describing an appeal to the emotions that is too contrived, blatant, or superficial. Appeals to the emotions may surely be all of those things. But they need not be any of them and certainly the term *pathos*, properly used, carries much the same meaning today as it did for the ancients, referring to any appeal to the emotions. Such appeals have a legitimate place in most forms of argumentation, given that our responses to experiences inevitably involve both heart and head; indeed, many would argue that the direction our reason takes is always informed at some level by our initial, emotional responses. Such appeals may take many forms. When you read Orwell's "Shooting an Elephant," you will likely be moved by the full sweep of the experience the writer is recounting. Toews's "A Father's Faith" is another example of a piece in which an appeal to *pathos* arguably runs throughout the essay. But appeals to *pathos* may be embedded even in very brief descriptions that have strong emotive content.

For Aristotle and other ancient Greek authorities, an appeal to *ethos* was one based on the character of the person presenting the argument, whether that might have to do with the speaker's position of authority, his or her perceived honesty, or other ethical virtues. In modern usage, *ethos* is still used to refer to the character of the person putting forward an argument, but there may be more factors that come into play today in determining this character. The idea of authority is a case in point. Though our society's more populist impulses may make us less inclined to judge the merits of a given argument on the basis of the writer's credentials, reputation still influences the willingness many of us have to extend faith to authors. When Roland Barthes begins "The World of Wrestling" with the bold, seemingly contradictory claim that "The virtue of all-in wrestling is that it is a spectacle of excess," we are in part inclined to give the thought credence, or extend some faith that it will in fact become sensible, because it comes from such an esteemed thinker. Similarly, the idea of virtue today is somewhat more complicated: it is now quite widely accepted that we do not in fact have reliable information as to the virtues—or lack thereof—of the writer of an essay. Yet we can gain a sense of whether a writer seems virtuous or not from any number of tiny cues—in the compassion we may sense in an author's treatment of a subject, or, by contrast, in his or her failure to judge others generously. What this means is that, generally speaking, appeals to *ethos* may be considered to rest on a wider range of characteristics today, for instance on our knowledge of a given speaker and the way in which speakers present themselves, or on the overall personality that we sense behind a particular piece of writing.

Unlike the structural elements of logical arguments (whether as set out according to the principles of classical rhetoric, or according to those of modern manuals for academic essay writing), the sorts of appeals that literary non-fiction makes (to *logos*, *pathos*, and *ethos*) are unlikely ever to follow one upon the other in a predictable order. Appeals to logic may alternate with appeals to emotion, just as narrative and descriptive and argumentative passages may be interspersed one with another. Such alternation is a continual feature of a number of the pieces of literary non-fiction included here, including those by Gourevitch, Toews, and Al-Solaylee. Arguments that are almost academic in their tone may alternate with paragraphs in which appeals to *ethos* and *pathos* come to the fore. There may be sudden turns; surprise is a strategy that we tend to associate with narrative fiction but also one that may feature prominently in literary non-fiction. Surprise may be said, for example, to be part of the structure of the Gourevitch piece, as it surely is of Toews's.

I end this introduction with one more glance in the direction of the two points of comparison we've used throughout: the principles of classical rhetoric and those of modern academic essay writing. Both those sets of principles are prescriptive: the precepts of classical rhetoric were designed to help orators organize and deliver their speeches in a methodical, articulate way. Similarly, modern manuals of essay writing are designed to help students follow the established conventions of an academic discipline. It is more difficult—perhaps impossible—to provide a blueprint for how to write literary non-fiction—and certainly this introduction makes no attempt to do so. It aims to be descriptive rather than prescriptive—to give some sense of the history and characteristics of the genre of literary non-fiction. While the selections here don't aim to trace the historical development of the genre, they do provide some sense of this burgeoning genre's diversity and versatility.

[P.L.]

Jonathan Swift
1667–1745

Although the art of literary satire traces its origins to antiquity, its golden age is often said to have occurred in the late seventeenth and eighteenth centuries—the time of Molière, Dryden, Pope, and Voltaire. Among the many gifted satirical minds that set out during this period to lash the vices and follies of mankind, none was more adept than Jonathan Swift, who aimed to "vex the world" into reform but acknowledged the limitations of satire as a "glass wherein beholders do generally discover everybody's face but their own."

Swift is best known as the author of *Gulliver's Travels* (1726), but he initially rose to prominence—first with the Whigs, then with the Tories—as one of the most brilliant political writers of his day. Ordained as a priest in the Anglican Church, Swift entertained hopes for ecclesiastical preferment in England, but when in 1714 the Tory ministry fell with the death of Queen Anne, he reluctantly retreated to his native Ireland, where he had been appointed dean of St. Patrick's Cathedral in Dublin. Here Swift came face to face with the appalling conditions of the Irish poor, whose hardships were much exacerbated by English economic policy. To this day Swift is regarded as a national hero for the many letters and pamphlets—published anonymously though their authorship was generally known—in which he championed Irish political and economic independence, discharging his "savage indignation" in some of the finest prose ever written.

Swift was moved to write much of his satire in response to particular events and circumstances, but the objects of his attack—above all the moral and intellectual failings of the human race—are perennial. "A Modest Proposal" (1729), his darkest, most disturbingly cynical work, appeared at the height of Ireland's wretchedness, a time of rampant inflation, poverty, famine, homelessness, and unemployment.

A Modest Proposal

For Preventing the Children of Poor People in Ireland from Being a Burden to Their Parents or the Country, and for Making Them Beneficial to the Public

It is a melancholy object to those who walk through this great town,[1] or travel in the country, when they see the streets, the roads, and cabin doors crowded with beggars of the female sex, followed by three, four, or six children, all in

[handwritten annotation: opening scene]

---

1   *this great town* I.e., Dublin.

rags and importuning every passenger[1] for an alms. These mothers, instead of being able to work for their honest livelihood, are forced to employ all their time in strolling[2] to beg sustenance for their helpless infants, who, as they grow up, either turn thieves for want of work, or leave their dear native country to fight for the Pretender in Spain, or sell themselves to the Barbados.[3]

I think it is agreed by all parties that this prodigious number of children in the arms, or on the backs, or at the heels of their mothers, and frequently of their fathers, is, in the present deplorable state of the kingdom, a very great additional grievance; and therefore, whoever could find out a fair, cheap, and easy method of making these children sound and useful members of the commonwealth would deserve so well of the public as to have his statue set up for a preserver of the nation.

But my intention is very far from being confined to provide only for the children of professed beggars; it is of a much greater extent, and shall take in the whole number of infants at a certain age who are born of parents in effect as little able to support them as those who demand our charity in the streets.

As to my own part, having turned my thoughts for many years upon this important subject and maturely weighed the several schemes of other projectors,[4] I have always found them grossly mistaken in their computation. 'Tis true, a child just dropped from its dam may be supported by her milk for a solar year with little other nourishment, at most not above the value of two shillings, which the mother may certainly get, or the value in scraps, by her lawful occupation of begging; and it is exactly at one year old that I propose to provide for them in such a manner as, instead of being a charge upon their parents or the parish, or wanting food and raiment for the rest of their lives, they shall on the contrary contribute to the feeding, and partly to the clothing, of many thousands.

There is likewise another great advantage in my scheme, that it will prevent those abortions, and that horrid practice of women murdering their bastard children, alas, too frequent among us, sacrificing the poor innocent babes, I doubt,[5] more to avoid the expense than the shame, which would move tears and pity in the most savage and inhuman breast.

1   *passenger* Passerby.
2   *strolling* Wandering, roving.
3   *the Pretender* James Francis Edward Stuart, son of James II who was deposed from the throne in the Glorious Revolution due to his overt Catholicism. Catholic Ireland was loyal to Stuart, and the Irish were often recruited by France and Spain to fight against England; *Barbados* Because of the extreme poverty in Ireland, many Irish people emigrated to the West Indies, selling their labour to sugar plantations in advance to pay for the voyage.
4   *projectors* Those who design or propose experiments or projects.
5   *doubt* Think.

The number of souls in this kingdom being usually reckoned one million and a half, of these I calculate there may be about two hundred thousand couples whose wives are breeders, from which number I subtract thirty thousand couples who are able to maintain children, although I apprehend there cannot be as many under the present distresses of the kingdom; but this being granted, there will remain one hundred and seventy thousand breeders.

I again subtract fifty thousand for those women who miscarry, or whose children die by accident or disease within the year. There only remain one hundred and twenty thousand children of poor parents annually born. The question therefore is how this number shall be reared and provided for, which, as I have already said, under the present situation of affairs is utterly impossible by all the methods hitherto proposed. For we can neither employ them in handicraft or agriculture; we neither build houses (I mean in the country) nor cultivate land.[1] They can very seldom pick up a livelihood by stealing till they arrive at six years old, except where they are of towardly parts,[2] although I confess they learn the rudiments much earlier, during which time they can however be properly looked upon only as probationers, as I have been informed by a principal gentleman in the county of Cavan, who protested to me that he never knew above one or two instances under the age of six, even in a part of the kingdom so renowned for the quickest proficiency in that art.

I am assured by our merchants that a boy or a girl before twelve years old is no saleable commodity; and even when they come to this age, they will not yield above three pounds, or three pounds and half a crown at most, on the Exchange, which cannot turn to account[3] either to the parents or the kingdom, the charge of nutriment and rags having been at least four times that value.

I shall now therefore humbly propose my own thoughts, which I hope will not be liable to the least objection.

I have been assured by a very knowing American[4] of my acquaintance in London that a young healthy child well nursed is at a year old a most delicious, nourishing, and wholesome food, whether stewed, roasted, baked, or boiled; and I make no doubt that it will equally serve in a fricassee or a ragout.[5]

I do therefore humbly offer it to public consideration that of the hundred and twenty thousand children already computed, twenty thousand may be

---

1 *neither build ... land* The British placed numerous restrictions on the Irish agricultural industry, retaining the majority of land for the grazing of sheep. The vast estates of British absentee landlords further contributed to Ireland's poverty.

2 *of towardly parts* Exceptionally able.

3 *on the Exchange* At the market; *turn to account* Result in profit.

4 *American* I.e., Native American.

5 *fricassee or a ragout* Stews.

reserved for breed, whereof only one fourth part to be males, which is more than we allow to sheep, black cattle, or swine, and my reason is that these children are seldom the fruits of marriage, a circumstance not much regarded by our savages; therefore, one male will be sufficient to serve four females. That the remaining hundred thousand may at a year old be offered in sale to the persons of quality and fortune through the kingdom, always advising the mother to let them suck plentifully of the last month, so as to render them plump and fat for a good table. A child will make two dishes at an entertainment for friends, and when the family dines alone, the fore or hind quarter will make a reasonable dish, and seasoned with a little pepper or salt will be very good boiled on the fourth day, especially in winter.

I have reckoned upon a medium that a child just born will weigh twelve pounds, and in a solar year if tolerably nursed increase to twenty-eight pounds.

I grant this food will be somewhat dear,[1] and therefore very proper for landlords, who, as they have already devoured most of the parents, seem to have the best title to the children.

Infants' flesh will be in season throughout the year, but more plentiful in March, and a little before and after. For we are told by a grave author, an eminent French physician, that, fish being a prolific[2] diet, there are more children born in Roman Catholic countries about nine months after Lent than at any other season; therefore, reckoning a year after Lent, the markets will be more glutted than usual because the number of popish[3] infants is at least three to one in this kingdom, and therefore it will have one other collateral advantage by lessening the number of papists among us.

I have already computed the charge of nursing a beggar's child (in which list I reckon all cottagers,[4] labourers, and four fifths of the farmers) to be about two shillings per annum, rags included, and I believe no gentleman would repine to give ten shillings for the carcass of a good fat child, which, as I have said, will make four dishes of excellent nutritive meat when he hath only some particular friend or his own family to dine with him. Thus the squire[5] will learn to be a good landlord and grow popular among his tenants; the mother will have eight shillings net profit and be fit for work till she produces another child.

---

1   *dear* Expensive.
2   *grave author* Sixteenth-century satirist François Rabelais. See his *Gargantua and Pantagruel; prolific* I.e., causing increased fertility.
3   *popish* Derogatory term meaning "Catholic."
4   *cottagers* Country dwellers.
5   *squire* Owner of a country estate.

Those who are more thrifty (as I must confess the times require) may flay the carcass, the skin of which, artificially[1] dressed, will make admirable gloves for ladies and summer boots for fine gentlemen.

As to our city of Dublin, shambles[2] may be appointed for this purpose in the most convenient parts of it, and butchers we may be assured will not be wanting, although I rather recommend buying the children alive and dressing them hot from the knife, as we do roasting pigs.

A very worthy person, a true lover of his country, and whose virtues I highly esteem, was lately pleased, in discoursing on this matter, to offer a refinement upon my scheme. He said that, many gentlemen of this kingdom having of late destroyed their deer, he conceived that the want of venison might be well supplied by the bodies of young lads and maidens, not exceeding fourteen years of age nor under twelve, so great a number of both sexes in every county being now ready to starve for want of work and service; and these to be disposed of by their parents if alive, or otherwise by their nearest relations. But with due deference to so excellent a friend and so deserving a patriot, I cannot be altogether in his sentiments; for as to the males, my American acquaintance assured me from frequent experience that their flesh was generally tough and lean, like that of our schoolboys, by continual exercise, and their taste disagreeable, and to fatten them would not answer the charge. Then as to the females, it would, I think with humble submission, be a loss to the public because they soon would become breeders themselves. And besides, it is not improbable that some scrupulous people might be apt to censure such a practice (although indeed very unjustly) as a little bordering upon cruelty, which, I confess, hath always been with me the strongest objection against any project, however well intended.

But in order to justify my friend, he confessed that this expedient was put into his head by the famous Psalmanazar,[3] a native of the island of Formosa, who came from thence to London above twenty years ago, and in conversation told my friend that in his country, when any young person happened to be put to death the executioner sold the carcass to persons of quality as a prime dainty, and that in his time the body of a plump girl of fifteen, who was crucified for an attempt to poison the emperor, was sold to his Imperial Majesty's Prime Minister of State and other great Mandarins of the court, in joints from the

---

1   *artificially* Artfully, skillfully.
2   *shambles* Slaughterhouses.
3   *Psalmanazar* George Psalmanazar, a French adventurer who pretended to be a Formosan and published an account of Formosan customs, *Historical and Geographical Description of Formosa* (1704), which was later exposed as fraudulent. The story Swift recounts here is found in the second edition of Psalmanazar's work.

gibbet,[1] at four hundred crowns. Neither indeed can I deny that if the same use were made of several plump young girls in this town who, without one single groat to their fortunes, cannot stir abroad without a chair,[2] and appear at the playhouse and assemblies in foreign fineries which they never will pay for, the kingdom would not be the worse.

Some persons of a desponding spirit are in great concern about that vast number of poor people who are aged, diseased, or maimed, and I have been desired to employ my thoughts what course may be taken to ease the nation of so grievous an encumbrance. But I am not in the least pain upon that matter because it is very well known that they are every day dying and rotting by cold and famine, and filth and vermin, as fast as can be reasonably expected. And as to the younger labourers, they are now in almost as hopeful a condition. They cannot get work, and consequently pine away for want of nourishment to a degree that if at any time they are accidentally hired to common labour, they have not strength to perform it; and thus the country and themselves are happily delivered from the evils to come.

I have too long digressed, and therefore shall return to my subject. I think the advantages by the proposal which I have made are obvious and many, as well as of the highest importance.

For first, as I have already observed, it would greatly lessen the number of papists, with whom we are yearly overrun, being the principal breeders of the nation as well as our most dangerous enemies, and who stay at home on purpose with a design to deliver the kingdom to the Pretender, hoping to take their advantage by the absence of so many good Protestants, who have chosen rather to leave their country than stay at home and pay tithes against their conscience to an Episcopal curate.[3]

Secondly, the poorer tenants will have something valuable of their own, which by law may be made liable to distress[4] and help to pay their landlord's rent, their corn and cattle being already seized, and money a thing unknown.

Thirdly, whereas the maintenance of an hundred thousand children from two years old and upwards cannot be computed at less than ten shillings apiece per annum, the nation's stock will be thereby increased fifty thousand pounds per annum, besides the profit of a new dish introduced to the tables of all gentlemen of fortune in the kingdom who have any refinement in taste,

---

1   *gibbet* Gallows.
2   *groat* Silver coin equal in value to four pence. It was removed from circulation in 1662, and thereafter "a groat" was used metaphorically to signify any very small sum; *chair* Sedan chair, which seated one person and was carried on poles by two men.
3   *Episcopal curate* I.e., Anglican church official.
4   *distress* Seizure of property for the payment of debt.

and the money will circulate among ourselves, the goods being entirely of our own growth and manufacture.

Fourthly, the constant breeders, besides the gain of eight shillings sterling per annum by the sale of their children, will be rid of the charge of maintaining them after the first year.

Fifthly, this food would likewise bring great customs to taverns, where the vintners will certainly be so prudent as to procure the best receipts[1] for dressing it to perfection, and consequently have their houses frequented by all the fine gentlemen who justly value themselves upon their knowledge in good eating. And a skillful cook who understands how to oblige his guests will contrive to make it as expensive as they please.

Sixthly, this would be a great inducement to marriage, which all wise nations have either encouraged by rewards or enforced by laws and penalties. It would increase the care and tenderness of mothers toward their children, when they were sure of a settlement for life to the poor babes, provided in some sort by the public, to their annual profit instead of expense. We should soon see an honest emulation[2] among the married women, which of them could bring the fattest child to market. Men would become as fond of their wives during the time of their pregnancy as they are now of their mares in foal, their cows in calf, or sows when they are ready to farrow, nor offer to beat or kick them (as it is too frequent a practice) for fear of a miscarriage.

Many other advantages might be enumerated: for instance, the addition of some thousand carcasses in our exportation of barrelled beef; the propagation of swine's flesh and improvement in the art of making good bacon, so much wanted among us by the great destruction of pigs, too frequent at our tables, which are no way comparable in taste or magnificence to a well-grown, fat yearling child, which, roasted whole, will make a considerable figure at a Lord Mayor's feast or any other public entertainment. But this and many others I omit, being studious of brevity.

Supposing that one thousand families in this city would be constant customers for infants' flesh, besides others who might have it at merry-meetings, particularly weddings and christenings, I compute that Dublin would take off annually about twenty thousand carcasses, and the rest of the kingdom (where probably they will be sold somewhat cheaper) the remaining eighty thousand.

I can think of no one objection that will possibly be raised against this proposal, unless it should be urged that the number of people will be thereby much lessened in the kingdom. This I freely own, and it was indeed one principal design in offering it to the world. I desire the reader will observe

---

1   *receipts* Recipes.
2   *emulation* Rivalry.

that I calculate my remedy for this one individual kingdom of Ireland, and for no other that ever was, is, or, I think, ever can be upon earth. Therefore let no man talk to me of other expedients:[1] of taxing our absentees at five shillings a pound; of using neither clothes nor household furniture, except what is of our own growth and manufacture; of utterly rejecting the materials and instruments that promote foreign luxury; of curing the expensiveness of pride, vanity, idleness, and gaming[2] in our women; of introducing a vein of parsimony, prudence, and temperance; of learning to love our country, wherein we differ even from Laplanders and the inhabitants of Topinamboo; of quitting our animosities and factions, nor act any longer like the Jews, who were murdering one another at the very moment their city was taken;[3] of being a little cautious not to sell our country and consciences for nothing; of teaching landlords to have at least one degree of mercy toward their tenants; lastly, of putting a spirit of honesty, industry, and skill into our shopkeepers, who, if a resolution could now be taken to buy only our native goods, would immediately unite to cheat and exact upon us in the price, the measure, and the goodness, nor could ever yet be brought to make one fair proposal of just dealing, though often in earnest invited to it.

Therefore I repeat, let no man talk to me of these and the like expedients till he hath at least some glimpse of hope that there will ever be some hearty and sincere attempt to put them in practice.

But as to myself, having been wearied out for many years with offering vain, idle, visionary thoughts, and at length utterly despairing of success, I fortunately fell upon this proposal, which, as it is wholly new, so it hath something solid and real, of no expense and little trouble, full in our own power, and whereby we can incur no danger in disobliging England. For this kind of commodity will not bear exportation, the flesh being of too tender a consistence to admit a long continuance in salt, although perhaps I could name a country[4] which would be glad to eat up our whole nation without it.

After all, I am not so violently bent upon my own opinion as to reject any offer, proposed by wise men, which shall be found equally innocent, cheap, easy, and effectual. But before something of that kind shall be advanced in

---

1   *other expedients* All of which Swift had already proposed in earnest attempts to remedy Ireland's poverty. See, for example, his *Proposal for the Universal Use of Irish Manufactures*. In early editions the following proposals were italicized to show the suspension of Swift's ironic tone.

2   *gaming* Gambling.

3   *Topinamboo* District in Brazil; *Jews ... was taken* According to the history of Flavius Josephus, Roman Emperor Titus's invasion and capture of Jerusalem in 70 BCE was aided by the fact that factional fighting had divided the city.

4   *a country* I.e., England.

contradiction to my scheme, and offering a better, I desire the author or authors will be pleased maturely to consider two points.

First, as things now stand, how they will be able to find food and raiment for one hundred thousand useless mouths and backs.

And secondly, there being a round million of creatures in human figure throughout this kingdom whose whole subsistence, put into a common stock, would leave them in debt two million of pounds sterling, adding those who are beggars by profession to the bulk of farmers, cottagers, and labourers with their wives and children, who are beggars in effect.

I desire those politicians who dislike my overture, and may perhaps be so bold to attempt an answer, that they will first ask the parents of these mortals whether they would not at this day think it a great happiness to have been sold for food at a year old in the manner I prescribe, and thereby have avoided such a perpetual scene of misfortunes as they have since gone through by the oppression of landlords, the impossibility of paying rent without money or trade, the want of common sustenance, with neither house nor clothes to cover them from the inclemencies of the weather, and the most inevitable prospect of entailing[1] the like or greater miseries upon their breed forever.

I profess in the sincerity of my heart that I have not the least personal interest in endeavoring to promote this necessary work, having no other motive than the public good of my country by advancing our trade, providing for infants, relieving the poor, and giving some pleasure to the rich. I have no children by which I can propose to get a single penny, the youngest being nine years old, and my wife past childbearing.

—1729

---

1 *entailing* Bestowing, conferring.

Percy Bysshe Shelley
1792–1822

A poet, thinker, and activist devoted to social reform and the overthrow of injustice, Percy Shelley was not only one of the most radical English Romantics but—as even the comparatively conservative Wordsworth acknowledged—"one of the best *artists* of us all ... in workmanship of style." Shelley's politics and poetics intersect in visionary works that seek to stimulate in the reader an awareness of a higher order of experience and greater forms of value than a materialist conception of the world can comprehend. His critics dismissed him as a reckless naïf with "a weak grasp upon the actual," but his idealism was bounded by his skepticism, and what he called his "dreams of what ought to be" take greater heed in his mature works of "the difficult and unbending realities of actual life."

For much of his life Shelley saw himself as a persecuted outcast. In light of his atheism and political views, his scandalous espousal of free love, and his sympathy for early democratic thinkers such as Thomas Paine and William Godwin, his work was often suppressed or attacked. Shelley was frequently on the defensive, not only with respect to his character and work but on behalf of poetry itself. His unfinished *Defence of Poetry* (1840), written to rebut a tongue-in-cheek essay in which his friend Thomas Love Peacock declared the art useless in the modern era of technological and scientific progress, remains an eloquent vindication of the transformative power of the "poetical faculty" and the social and moral role of the poet.

from *A Defence of Poetry, or Remarks Suggested by an Essay Entitled "The Four Ages of Poetry"*[1]

According to one mode of regarding those two classes of mental action which are called reason and imagination, the former may be considered as mind con-

---

1   *A Defence ... Ages of Poetry* This essay, begun in 1822 and never completed, was written in response to an 1820 essay by Shelley's friend Thomas Love Peacock called "The Four Ages of Poetry." In this partially ironic essay, Peacock describes four cycles through which poetry passes: the first is an iron age of crude folk ballads, medieval romances, etc.; the second, the gold age, contains the great epics of Homer, Dante, and Milton; the third, the silver age, contains the "derivative" poetry of the Augustan poets (who included John Dryden and Alexander Pope); and the fourth stage, the age of brass, is that of Peacock's contemporaries, whom he claimed were markedly inferior. Criticizing Romantic poets such as Byron, Coleridge, and Wordsworth, Peacock urged the men of his generation to apply themselves to new sciences, such as astronomy, economics, politics, mathematics,

templating the relations borne by one thought to another, however produced; and the latter, as mind acting upon those thoughts so as to colour them with its own light, and composing from them, as from elements, other thoughts, each containing within itself the principle of its own integrity. The one is the τὸ ποιειω,[1] or the principle of synthesis, and has for its objects those forms which are common to universal nature and existence itself; the other is the τὸ λογιζειω[2] or principle of analysis, and its action regards the relations of things, simply as relations; considering thoughts, not in their integral unity, but as the algebraical representations which conduct to certain general results. Reason is the enumeration of quantities already known; imagination is the perception of the value of those quantities, both separately and as a whole. Reason respects the differences, and imagination the similitudes of things. Reason is to Imagination as the instrument to the agent, as the body to the spirit, as the shadow to the substance.

Poetry, in a general sense, may be defined to be "the expression of the Imagination": and poetry is connate with the origin of man. Man is an instrument over which a series of external and internal impressions are driven, like the alternations of an ever-changing wind over an Æolian lyre,[3] which move it by their motion to ever-changing melody. But there is a principle within the human being, and perhaps within all sentient beings, which acts otherwise than in the lyre, and produces not melody alone, but harmony, by an internal adjustment of the sounds or motions thus excited to the impressions which excite them. It is as if the lyre could accommodate its chords to the motions of that which strikes them, in a determined proportion of sound; even as the musician can accommodate his voice to the sound of the lyre. A child at play by itself will express its delight by its voice and motions; and every inflexion of tone and every gesture will bear exact relation to a corresponding antitype in the pleasurable impressions which awakened it; it will be the reflected image of that impression; and as the lyre trembles and sounds after the wind has died away, so the child seeks, by prolonging in its voice and motions the duration of the effect, to prolong also a consciousness of the cause. In relation to the objects which delight a child, these expressions are what poetry is to higher objects. The savage (for the savage is to ages what the child is to years) expresses

---

or chemistry, instead of poetry. Though Shelley recognized Peacock's satirical humour, he also acknowledged that Peacock had put his finger on a common bias of the time—both in the theories of Utilitarian philosophers and in general public opinion—in favour of economic growth and scientific progress over creativity and humanitarian concerns. It was this bias that he attempted to correct in his *Defence*.

1   τὸ ποιειω Greek: making.
2   τὸ λογιζειω Greek: reasoning.
3   *Æolian lyre* Stringed instrument that produces music when exposed to wind.

the emotions produced in him by surrounding objects in a similar manner; and language and gesture, together with plastic[1] or pictorial imitation, become the image of the combined effect of those objects, and of his apprehension of them. Man in society, with all his passions and his pleasures, next becomes the object of the passions and pleasures of man; an additional class of emotions produces an augmented treasure of expressions; and language, gesture, and the imitative arts become at once the representation and the medium, the pencil and the picture, the chisel and the statue, the chord and the harmony. The social sympathies, or those laws from which as from its elements society results, begin to develop themselves from the moment that two human beings coexist; the future is contained within the present as the plant within the seed; and equality, diversity, unity, contrast, mutual dependence, become the principles alone capable of affording the motives according to which the will of a social being is determined to action, inasmuch as he is social; and constitute pleasure in sensation, virtue in sentiment, beauty in art, truth in reasoning, and love in the intercourse of kind. Hence men, even in the infancy of society, observe a certain order in their words and actions, distinct from that of the objects and the impressions represented by them, all expression being subject to the laws of that from which it proceeds. But let us dismiss those more general considerations which might involve an enquiry into the principles of society itself, and restrict our view to the manner in which the imagination is expressed upon its forms.

In the youth of the world, men dance and sing and imitate natural objects, observing[2] in these actions, as in all others, a certain rhythm or order. And, although all men observe a similar, they observe not the same order, in the motions of the dance, in the melody of the song, in the combinations of language, in the series of their imitations of natural objects. For there is a certain order or rhythm belonging to each of these classes of mimetic representation, from which the hearer and the spectator receive an intenser and purer pleasure than from any other: the sense of an approximation to this order has been called taste, by modern writers. Every man in the infancy of art observes an order which approximates more or less closely to that from which this highest delight results: but the diversity is not sufficiently marked, as that its gradations should be sensible, except in those instances where the predominance of this faculty of approximation to the beautiful (for so we may be permitted to name the relation between this highest pleasure and its cause) is very great. Those in whom it exists in excess are poets, in the most universal sense of the word; and the pleasure resulting from the manner in which they express the influence of

---

1   *plastic* I.e., sculptural.
2   *observing* Following.

society or nature upon their own minds, communicates itself to others, and gathers a sort of reduplication from that community. Their language is vitally metaphorical; that is, it marks the before unapprehended relations of things, and perpetuates their apprehension, until the words which represent them, become through time signs for portions or classes of thoughts instead of pictures of integral thoughts; and then if no new poets should arise to create afresh the associations which have been thus disorganized, language will be dead to all the nobler purposes of human intercourse. These similitudes or relations are finely said by Lord Bacon to be "the same footsteps of nature impressed upon the various subjects of the world"[1]—and he considers the faculty which perceives them as the storehouse of axioms common to all knowledge. In the infancy of society every author is necessarily a poet, because language itself is poetry; and to be a poet is to apprehend the true and the beautiful, in a word the good which exists in the relation, subsisting, first between existence and perception, and secondly between perception and expression. Every original language near to its source is in itself the chaos of a cyclic poem:[2] the copiousness of lexicography and the distinctions of grammar are the works of a later age, and are merely the catalogue and the form of the creations of Poetry.

But Poets, or those who imagine and express this indestructible order, are not only the authors of language and of music, of the dance and architecture and statuary and painting: they are the institutors of laws, and the founders of civil society and the inventors of the arts of life and the teachers, who draw into a certain propinquity with the beautiful and the true that partial apprehension of the agencies of the invisible world which is called religion. Hence all original religions are allegorical, or susceptible of allegory, and like Janus have a double face of false and true.[3] Poets, according to the circumstances of the age and nation in which they appeared, were called in the earlier epochs of the world legislators or prophets:[4] a poet essentially comprises and unites both these characters. For he not only beholds intensely the present as it is, and discovers those laws according to which present things ought to be ordered, but he beholds the future in the present, and his thoughts are the germs of the flower and the fruit of latest time. Not that I assert poets to be prophets in the gross sense of the word, or that they can foretell the form as surely as

---

1   *the same ... world* From Francis Bacon's *Of the Advancement of Learning* (1605) 3.1.

2   *cyclic poem* Set of poems dealing with the same subject (though not always by the same author). The "Arthurian Cycle," a series of poems about the court of King Arthur, is one example of the genre.

3   *like Janus ... true* Janus, the Roman god of war, of doorways, and of beginnings and endings, is generally depicted with two faces, one looking forward and one back.

4   *were called ... prophets* See Sir Philip Sidney's *Defence of Poesy* (1595), in which he points out that *vates*, the Latin word for poet, also means diviner or prophet.

they foreknow the spirit of events: such is the pretence of superstition which would make poetry an attribute of prophecy, rather than prophecy an attribute of poetry. A Poet participates in the eternal, the infinite, and the one; as far as relates to his conceptions, time and place and number are not. The grammatical forms which express the moods of time, and the difference of persons and the distinction of place, are convertible with respect to the highest poetry without injuring it as poetry, and the choruses of Æschylus, and the book of Job, and Dante's Paradise[1] would afford, more than any other writings, examples of this fact, if the limits of this essay did not forbid citation. The creations of sculpture, painting, and music are illustrations still more decisive.

Language, colour, form, and religious and civil habits of action are all the instruments and materials of poetry; they may be called poetry by that figure of speech which considers the effect as a synonym of the cause. But poetry in a more restricted sense expresses those arrangements of language, and especially metrical language, which are created by that imperial faculty whose throne is curtained within the invisible nature of man. And this springs from the nature itself of language, which is a more direct representation of the actions and passions of our internal being, and is susceptible of more various and delicate combinations, than colour, form, or motion, and is more plastic and obedient to the control of that faculty of which it is the creation. For language is arbitrarily produced by the Imagination and has relation to thoughts alone; but all other materials, instruments and conditions of art, have relations among each other, which limit and interpose between conception and expression. The former is as a mirror which reflects, the latter as a cloud which enfeebles, the light of which both are mediums of communication. Hence the fame of sculptors, painters and musicians, although the intrinsic powers of the great masters of these arts, may yield in no degree to that of those who have employed language as the hieroglyphic of their thoughts, has never equalled that of poets in the restricted sense of the term; as two performers of equal skill will produce unequal effects from a guitar and a harp. The fame of legislators and founders of religions, so long as their institutions last, alone seems to exceed that of poets in the restricted sense; but it can scarcely be a question whether, if we deduct the celebrity which their flattery of the gross opinions of the vulgar usually conciliates, together with that which belonged to them in their higher character of poets, any excess will remain.

We have thus circumscribed the meaning of the word Poetry within the limits of that art which is the most familiar and the most perfect expression of

---

1   *Æschylus* Greek tragic dramatist (c. 525–456 BCE); *Dante's Paradise* Reference to Italian poet Dante Alighieri's fourteenth-century work *The Divine Comedy*, which describes a journey from Hell, through Purgatory, to Paradise.

the faculty itself. It is necessary however to make the circle still narrower, and to determine the distinction between measured and unmeasured language; for the popular division into prose and verse is inadmissible in accurate philosophy. Sounds as well as thoughts have relation both between each other and towards that which they represent, and a perception of the order of those relations has always been found connected with a perception of the order of the relations of thoughts. Hence the language of poets has ever affected a certain uniform and harmonious recurrence of sound, without which it were not poetry, and which is scarcely less indispensable to the communication of its influence, than the words themselves, without reference to that peculiar order....

A poem is the very image of life expressed in its eternal truth. There is this difference between a story and a poem, that a story is a catalogue of detached facts, which have no other bond of connection than time, place, circumstance, cause and effect; the other is the creation of actions according to the unchangeable forms of human nature, as existing in the mind of the creator, which is itself the image of all other minds. The one is partial, and applies only to a definite period of time, and a certain combination of events which can never again recur; the other is universal, and contains within itself the germ of a relation to whatever motives or actions have place in the possible varieties of human nature....

Poetry is ever accompanied with pleasure: all spirits on which it falls open themselves to receive the wisdom which is mingled with its delight. In the infancy of the world, neither poets themselves nor their auditors are fully aware of the excellence of poetry: for it acts in a divine and unapprehended manner, beyond and above consciousness; and it is reserved for future generations to contemplate and measure the mighty cause and effect in all the strength and splendour of their union. Even in modern times, no living poet ever arrived at the fullness of his fame; the jury which sits in judgment upon a poet, belonging as he does to all time, must be composed of his peers: it must be impanelled by Time from the selectest of the wise of many generations. A Poet is a nightingale, who sits in darkness and sings to cheer its own solitude with sweet sounds; his auditors are as men entranced by the melody of an unseen musician, who feel that they are moved and softened, yet know not whence or why. The poems of Homer and his contemporaries were the delight of infant Greece; they were the elements of that social system which is the column upon which all succeeding civilization has reposed. Homer embodied the ideal perfection of his age in human character; nor can we doubt that those who read his verses were awakened to an ambition of becoming like to Achilles, Hector and Ulysses:[1] the truth and beauty of friendship, patriotism, and persevering devotion to an

---

1   *Achilles, Hector and Ulysses* Trojan and Greek heroes in Homer's *Iliad* and *Odyssey*.

object were unveiled to the depths in these immortal creations: the sentiments of the auditors must have been refined and enlarged by a sympathy with such great and lovely impersonations, until from admiring they imitated, and from imitation they identified themselves with the objects of their admiration....

The whole objection, however, of the immorality of poetry[1] rests upon a misconception of the manner in which poetry acts to produce the moral improvement of man. Ethical science[2] arranges the elements which poetry has created, and propounds schemes and proposes examples of civil and domestic life: nor is it for want of admirable doctrines that men hate, and despise, and censure, and deceive, and subjugate one another. But Poetry acts in another and diviner manner. It awakens and enlarges the mind itself by rendering it the receptacle of a thousand unapprehended combinations of thought. Poetry lifts the veil from the hidden beauty of the world, and makes familiar objects be as if they were not familiar; it reproduces all that it represents, and the impersonations clothed in its Elysian[3] light stand thenceforward in the minds of those who have once contemplated them, as memorials of that gentle and exalted content which extends itself over all thoughts and actions with which it coexists. The great secret of morals is Love; or a going out of our own nature, and an identification of ourselves with the beautiful which exists in thought, action, or person not our own. A man, to be greatly good, must imagine intensely and comprehensively; he must put himself in the place of another and of many others; the pains and pleasures of his species must become his own. The great instrument of moral good is the imagination; and poetry administers to the effect by acting upon the cause. Poetry enlarges the circumference of the imagination by replenishing it with thoughts of ever new delight, which have the power of attracting and assimilating to their own nature all other thoughts, and which form new intervals and interstices whose void for ever craves fresh food. Poetry strengthens that faculty which is the organ of the moral nature of man, in the same manner as exercise strengthens a limb. A Poet therefore would do ill to embody his own conceptions of right and wrong, which are usually those of his place and time, in his poetical creations, which participate in neither. By this assumption of the inferior office of interpreting the effect, in which perhaps after all he might acquit himself but imperfectly, he would resign the glory in a participation in the cause. There was little danger that Homer, or any of the eternal poets, should have so far misunderstood themselves as to have abdicated this throne of their widest dominion. Those

---

1   *immorality of poetry* An objection voiced by Plato in his *Republic*, in which he says that poetry often depicts characters who are morally imperfect and whose actions do not provide suitable examples for readers.

2   *Ethical science* Moral philosophy.

3   *reproduces* I.e., produces or creates anew; *Elysian* I.e., of paradise.

in whom the poetical faculty, though great, is less intense, as Euripides, Lucan, Tasso, Spenser,[1] have frequently affected a moral aim, and the effect of their poetry is diminished in exact proportion to the degree in which they compel us to advert to this purpose....

The drama at Athens, or wheresoever else it may have approached to its perfection, coexisted with the moral and intellectual greatness of the age. The tragedies of the Athenian poets are as mirrors in which the spectator beholds himself, under a thin disguise of circumstance, stript of all but that ideal perfection and energy which every one feels to be the internal type of all that he loves, admires, and would become. The imagination is enlarged by a sympathy with pains and passions so mighty that they distend in their conception the capacity of that by which they are conceived; the good affections are strengthened by pity, indignation, terror and sorrow; and an exalted calm is prolonged from the satiety of this high exercise of them into the tumult of familiar life; even crime is disarmed of half its horror and all its contagion by being represented as the fatal consequence of the unfathomable agencies of nature; error is thus divested of its willfulness; men can no longer cherish it as the creation of their choice. In a drama of the highest order there is little food for censure or hatred; it teaches rather self-knowledge and self-respect. Neither the eye nor the mind can see itself, unless reflected upon that which it resembles. The drama, so long as it continues to express poetry, is as a prismatic and many-sided mirror, which collects the brightest rays of human nature and divides and reproduces them from the simplicity of these elementary forms, and touches them with majesty and beauty, and multiplies all that it reflects, and endows it with the power of propagating its like wherever it may fall.

But in periods of the decay of social life, the drama sympathizes with that decay. Tragedy becomes a cold imitation of the form of the great masterpieces of antiquity, divested of all harmonious accompaniment of the kindred arts; and often the very form misunderstood: or a weak attempt to teach certain doctrines, which the writer considers as moral truths; and which are usually no more than specious flatteries of some gross vice or weakness with which the author in common with his auditors are infected....

The drama being that form under which a greater number of modes of expression of poetry are susceptible of being combined than any other, the connection of poetry and social good is more observable in the drama than in whatever other form: and it is indisputable that the highest perfection of human society has ever corresponded with the highest dramatic excellence;

---

1   *Euripides* Greek tragedian of the fifth century BCE; *Lucan* Roman poet of the first century CE; *Tasso* Torquato Tasso, Italian epic poet of the sixteenth century; *Spenser* Edmund Spenser, sixteenth-century epic poet; author of *The Faerie Queene*.

and that the corruption or the extinction of the drama in a nation where it has once flourished, is a mark of a corruption of manners, and an extinction of the energies which sustain the soul of social life. But, as Machiavelli[1] says of political institutions, that life may be preserved and renewed, if men should arise capable of bringing back the drama to its principles. And this is true with respect to poetry in its most extended sense: all language, institution and form, require not only to be produced but to be sustained: the office and character of a poet participates in the divine nature as regards providence, no less than as regards creation.

… It is admitted that the exercise of the imagination is most delightful, but it is alleged that that of reason is more useful. Let us examine as the grounds of this distinction, what is here meant by Utility. Pleasure or good, in a general sense, is that which the consciousness of a sensitive and intelligent being seeks, and in which when found it acquiesces. There are two kinds of pleasure, one durable, universal, and permanent; the other transitory and particular. Utility may either express the means of producing the former or the latter. In the former sense, whatever strengthens and purifies the affections, enlarges the imagination, and adds spirit to sense, is useful. But the meaning in which the Author of the Four Ages of Poetry seems to have employed the word utility is the narrower one of banishing the importunity of the wants of our animal nature, the surrounding men with security of life, the dispersing the grosser delusions of superstition, and the conciliating such a degree of mutual forbearance among men as may consist with the motives of personal advantage.

Undoubtedly the promoters of utility in this limited sense have their appointed office in society. They follow the footsteps of poets, and copy the sketches of their creations into the book of common life. They make space, and give time. Their exertions are of the highest value so long as they confine their administration of the concerns of the inferior powers of our nature within the limits due to the superior ones. But whilst the skeptic destroys gross superstitions, let him spare to deface, as some of the French writers have defaced, the eternal truths charactered upon the imaginations of men. Whilst the mechanist abridges, and the political economist combines, labour, let them beware that their speculations, for want of correspondence with those first principles which belong to the imagination, do not tend, as they have in modern England, to exasperate at once the extremes of luxury and want. They have exemplified the saying, "To him that hath, more shall be given; and from him that hath not,

---

1   *Machiavelli* Niccolò Machiavelli (1469–1527), author of the political treatise *The Prince*.

the little that he hath shall be taken away."[1] The rich have become richer, and the poor have become poorer; and the vessel of the state is driven between the Scylla and Charybdis[2] of anarchy and despotism. Such are the effects which must ever flow from an unmitigated exercise of the calculating faculty.

It is difficult to define pleasure in its highest sense; the definition involving a number of apparent paradoxes. For, from an inexplicable defect of harmony in the constitution of human nature, the pain of the inferior is frequently connected with the pleasures of the superior portions of our being. Sorrow, terror, anguish, despair itself are often the chosen expressions of an approximation to the highest good. Our sympathy in tragic fiction depends on this principle; tragedy delights by affording a shadow of the pleasure which exists in pain. This is the source also of the melancholy which is inseparable from the sweetest melody. The pleasure that is in sorrow is sweeter than the pleasure of pleasure itself. And hence the saying, "It is better to go to the house of mourning, than to the house of mirth."[3] Not that this highest species of pleasure is necessarily linked with pain. The delight of love and friendship, the ecstasy of the admiration of nature, the joy of the perception and still more of the creation of poetry is often wholly unalloyed.

The production and assurance of pleasure in this highest sense is true utility. Those who produce and preserve this pleasure are Poets or poetical philosophers.

The exertions of Locke, Hume, Gibbon, Voltaire, Rousseau,[4] and their disciples, in favour of oppressed and deluded humanity, are entitled to the gratitude of mankind. Yet it is easy to calculate the degree of moral and intellectual improvement which the world would have exhibited, had they never lived. A little more nonsense would have been talked for a century or two; and perhaps a few more men, women, and children, burnt as heretics. We might not at this moment have been congratulating each other on the abolition of the Inquisition in Spain.[5] But it exceeds all imagination to conceive what would have been the moral condition of the world if neither Dante, Petrarch, Boccaccio, Chaucer, Shakespeare, Calderon, Lord Bacon, nor Milton, had ever

---

1   *To him ... away* Repeatedly said by Jesus (Matthew 25.29, Mark 4.25, Luke 8.18 and 19.26).

2   *Scylla and Charybdis* A group of rocks and a whirlpool located at the Strait of Messina (between Sicily and mainland Italy).

3   *It is ... mirth* From Ecclesiastes 7.2.

4   *Locke ... Rousseau* John Locke, David Hume, Edward Gibbon, François-Marie Arouet Voltaire, and Jean-Jacques Rousseau, noted philosophers of the seventeenth and eighteenth centuries.

5   *We might ... Spain* The Inquisition was suspended in 1820, the year before Shelley wrote this essay, and abolished permanently in 1834.

existed; if Raphael and Michael Angelo[1] had never been born; if the Hebrew poetry had never been translated; if a revival of the study of Greek literature had never taken place; if no monuments of ancient sculpture had been handed down to us; and if the poetry of the religion of the ancient world had been extinguished together with its belief. The human mind could never, except by the intervention of these excitements, have been awakened to the invention of the grosser sciences, and that application of analytical reasoning to the aberrations of society, which it is now attempted to exalt over the direct expression of the inventive and creative faculty itself.

... The cultivation of those sciences which have enlarged the limits of the empire of man over the external world, has, for want of the poetical faculty, proportionally circumscribed those of the internal world; and man, having enslaved the elements, remains himself a slave. To what but a cultivation of the mechanical arts in a degree disproportioned to the presence of the creative faculty, which is the basis of all knowledge, is to be attributed the abuse of all invention for abridging and combining labour, to the exasperation of the inequality of mankind? From what other cause has it arisen that the discoveries which should have lightened, have added a weight to the curse imposed on Adam?[2] Poetry, and the principle of Self, of which money is the visible incarnation, are the God and the Mammon of the world.[3]

The functions of the poetical faculty are two-fold; by one it creates new materials of knowledge, and power and pleasure; by the other it engenders in the mind a desire to reproduce and arrange them according to a certain rhythm and order which may be called the beautiful and the good. The cultivation of poetry is never more to be desired than at periods when, from an excess of the selfish and calculating principle, the accumulation of the materials of external life exceed the quantity of the power of assimilating them to the internal laws of human nature. The body has then become too unwieldy for that which animates it.

Poetry is indeed something divine. It is at once the centre and circumference of knowledge; it is that which comprehends all science, and that to which all science must be referred. It is at the same time the root and blossom of all other systems of thought: it is that from which all spring, and that which

---

1   *Petrarch* Fourteenth-century Italian poet, best known for developing the Italian/ Petrarchan sonnet; *Boccaccio* Italian poet, author of the *Decameron* (1351–53); *Calderon* Seventeenth-century Spanish poet and dramatist; *Raphael and Michael Angelo* Italian Renaissance painters.

2   *curse imposed on Adam* Adam is cursed to labour for his food; see Genesis 3.17–19.

3   *God and ... world* See Matthew 6.24: "No man can serve two masters: for either he will hate the one, and love the other; or else he will hold to the one, and despise the other. Ye cannot serve God and Mammon," Mammon being the false idol of worldly possessions.

adorns all; and that which, if blighted, denies the fruit and the seed, and withholds from the barren world the nourishment and the succession of the scions[1] of the tree of life. It is the perfect and consummate surface and bloom of things; it is as the odour and the colour of the rose to the texture of the elements which compose it, as the form and the splendour of unfaded beauty to the secrets of anatomy and corruption. What were Virtue, Love, Patriotism, Friendship &c.—what were the scenery of this beautiful Universe which we inhabit—what were our consolations on this side of the grave—and what were our aspirations beyond it—if Poetry did not ascend to bring light and fire from those eternal regions where the owl-winged faculty of calculation dare not ever soar? Poetry is not like reasoning, a power to be exerted according to the determination of the will. A man cannot say, "I will compose poetry." The greatest poet even cannot say it: for the mind in creation is as a fading coal which some invisible influence, like an inconstant wind, awakens to transitory brightness: this power arises from within, like the colour of a flower which fades and changes as it is developed, and the conscious portions of our natures are unprophetic either of its approach or its departure....

Poetry is the record of the best and happiest moments of the happiest and best minds. We are aware of evanescent visitations of thought and feeling sometimes associated with place or person, sometimes regarding our own mind alone, and always arising unforeseen and departing unbidden, but elevating and delightful beyond all expression: so that even in the desire and the regret they leave, there cannot but be pleasure, participating as it does in the nature of its object. It is as it were the interpenetration of a diviner nature through our own; but its footsteps are like those of a wind over a sea, which the coming calm erases, and whose traces remain only as on the wrinkled sand which paves it. These and corresponding conditions of being are experienced principally by those of the most delicate sensibility and the most enlarged imagination; and the state of mind produced by them is at war with every base desire. The enthusiasm of virtue, love, patriotism, and friendship is essentially linked with these emotions; and whilst they last, self appears as what it is, an atom to a Universe. Poets are not only subject to these experiences as spirits of the most refined organization, but they can colour all that they combine with the evanescent hues of this ethereal world; a word, a trait in the representation of a scene or a passion, will touch the enchanted chord, and reanimate, in those who have ever experienced these emotions, the sleeping, the cold, the buried image of the past. Poetry thus makes immortal all that is best and most beautiful in the world; it arrests the vanishing apparitions which haunt

---

1   *scions* Shoots.

the interlunations[1] of life, and veiling them or in language or in form sends them forth among mankind, bearing sweet news of kindred joy to those with whom their sisters abide—abide, because there is no portal of expression from the caverns of the spirit which they inhabit into the universe of things. Poetry redeems from decay the visitations of the divinity in man.

Poetry turns all things to loveliness; it exalts the beauty of that which is most beautiful, and it adds beauty to that which is most deformed: it marries exultation and horror, grief and pleasure, eternity and change; it subdues to union under its light yoke all irreconcilable things. It transmutes all that it touches, and every form moving within the radiance of its presence is changed by wondrous sympathy to an incarnation of the spirit which it breathes; its secret alchemy turns to potable[2] gold the poisonous waters which flow from death through life; it strips the veil of familiarity from the world, and lays bare the naked and sleeping beauty which is the spirit of its forms.

All things exist as they are perceived: at least in relation to the percipient. "The mind is its own place, and of itself can make a heaven of hell, a hell of heaven."[3] But poetry defeats the curse which binds us to be subjected to the accident of surrounding impressions. And whether it spreads its own figured curtain or withdraws life's dark veil from before the scene of things, it equally creates for us a being within our being. It makes us the inhabitants of a world to which the familiar world is a chaos. It reproduces the common universe of which we are portions and percipients, and it purges from our inward sight the film of familiarity which obscures from us the wonder of our being. It compels us to feel that which we perceive, and to imagine that which we know. It creates anew the universe after it has been annihilated in our minds by the recurrence of impressions blunted by reiteration....

The first part of these remarks has related to Poetry in its elements and principles; and it has been shown, as well as the narrow limits assigned them would permit, that what is called poetry, in a restricted sense, has a common source with all other forms of order and of beauty according to which the materials of human life are susceptible of being arranged, and which is poetry in an universal sense.

The second part[4] will have for its object an application of these principles to the present state of the cultivation of Poetry, and a defence of the attempt to idealize the modern forms of manners and opinion, and compel them into a subordination to the imaginative and creative faculty. For the

1   *interlunations* Periods between old and new moons; periods of darkness.
2   *potable* Drinkable. Alchemists sought a liquid form of gold that, when consumed, would be the elixir of life.
3   *The mind ... heaven* From Satan's speech in Milton's *Paradise Lost* 1.254–55.
4   *The second part* Shelley did not complete a second part.

literature of England, an energetic development of which has ever preceded or accompanied a great and free development of the national will, has arisen as it were from a new birth. In spite of the low-thoughted envy which would undervalue contemporary merit, our own will be a memorable age in intellectual achievements, and we live among such philosophers and poets as surpass beyond comparison any who have appeared since the last national struggle for civil and religious liberty.[1] The most unfailing herald, companion, and follower of the awakening of a great people to work a beneficial change in opinion or institution, is Poetry. At such periods there is an accumulation of the power of communicating and receiving intense and impassioned conceptions respecting man and nature. The persons in whom this power resides, may often, as far as regards many portions of their nature, have little apparent correspondence with that spirit of good of which they are the ministers. But even whilst they deny and abjure, they are yet compelled to serve the Power which is seated upon the throne of their own soul. It is impossible to read the compositions of the most celebrated writers of the present day without being startled with the electric life which burns within their words. They measure the circumference and sound the depths of human nature with a comprehensive and all-penetrating spirit, and they are themselves perhaps the most sincerely astonished at its manifestations, for it is less their spirit than the spirit of the age. Poets are the hierophants[2] of an unapprehended inspiration, the mirrors of the gigantic shadows which futurity casts upon the present, the words which express what they understand not; the trumpets which sing to battle, and feel not what they inspire: the influence which is moved not, but moves.[3] Poets are the unacknowledged legislators of the World.

—1820

---

1   *the last … liberty* I.e., the English Civil War of the 1640s.
2   *hierophants* Interpreters of sacred mysteries.
3   *is moved … moves* Reference to Greek philosopher Aristotle's concept of the "Unmoved Mover" of the universe.

Mark Twain (Samuel Clemens)
1835–1910

Samuel Clemens spent his childhood on the banks of the Mississippi River. His pen name comes from a term used on the Mississippi to refer to the second mark on the line that measured the depth of the water—mark twain, or the two-fathom mark, was a safe depth for steamboats. His childhood adventures and life on the river also provided the background for his most popular and enduring works.

After a chequered career that included stints as a printer's apprentice, steamboat pilot, soldier, miner, and provisional governor of the territory of Nevada, Clemens began to write as "Mark Twain." His reputation as a humourist grew as he gave public lectures and published articles, travel letters, and his first book of tales, *The Celebrated Jumping Frog of Calaveras County, and other Sketches* (1867). His fame was established when an assignment to travel to Europe and the Middle East resulted in the irreverent and witty *The Innocents Abroad* (1869).

After his marriage, Twain settled down and wrote prolifically for the rest of his life, although he also undertook tours to give humourous and satirical lectures, such as "Advice to Youth" (1882). He set two novels, *The Prince and the Pauper* (1882) and *A Connecticut Yankee in King Arthur's Court* (1889), in England, but is best known for the two novels set in Twain's home state of Missouri: *The Adventures of Tom Sawyer* (1876) and *The Adventures of Huckleberry Finn* (1884). Ernest Hemingway famously said, "All modern American literature comes from one book by Mark Twain called *Huckleberry Finn*." Despite such critical admiration, this book has often generated controversy—as may be inevitable for any work that attempts to deal directly with issues of race and slavery in America.

Twain's writing continues to be highly regarded for its wit and satire, its lively depictions of Western life, and its effective use of vernacular language.

Advice to Youth

Being told I would be expected to talk here, I inquired what sort of talk I ought to make. They said it should be something suitable to youth—something didactic, instructive, or something in the nature of good advice. Very well. I have a few things in my mind which I have often longed to say for the instruction of the young; for it is in one's tender early years that such things will best take root and be most enduring and most valuable. First, then, I will say to you, my young friends—and I say it beseechingly, urgingly—

Always obey your parents, when they are present. This is the best policy in the long run, because if you don't they will make you. Most parents think they know better than you do, and you can generally make more by humouring that superstition than you can by acting on your own better judgment.

Be respectful to your superiors, if you have any, also to strangers, and sometimes to others. If a person offend you, and you are in doubt as to whether it was intentional or not, do not resort to extreme measures; simply watch your chance and hit him with a brick. That will be sufficient. If you shall find that he had not intended any offence, come out frankly and confess yourself in the wrong when you struck him; acknowledge it like a man and say you didn't mean to. Yes, always avoid violence; in this age of charity and kindliness, the time has gone by for such things. Leave dynamite to the low and unrefined.

Go to bed early, get up early—this is wise. Some authorities say get up with the sun; some others say get up with one thing, some with another. But a lark is really the best thing to get up with. It gives you a splendid reputation with everybody to know that you get up with the lark; and if you get the right kind of lark, and work at him right, you can easily train him to get up at half past nine, every time—it is no trick at all.

Now as to the matter of lying. You want to be very careful about lying; otherwise you are nearly sure to get caught. Once caught, you can never again be, in the eyes to the good and the pure, what you were before. Many a young person has injured himself permanently through a single clumsy and ill-finished lie, the result of carelessness born of incomplete training. Some authorities hold that the young ought not to lie at all. That, of course, is putting it rather stronger than necessary; still, while I cannot go quite so far as that, I do maintain, and I believe I am right, that the young ought to be temperate in the use of this great art until practice and experience shall give them that confidence, elegance, and precision which alone can make the accomplishment graceful and profitable. Patience, diligence, painstaking attention to detail—these are requirements; these, in time, will make the student perfect; upon these, and upon these only, may he rely as the sure foundation for future eminence. Think what tedious years of study, thought, practice, experience, went to the equipment of that peerless old master who was able to impose upon the whole world the lofty and sounding maxim that "truth is mighty and will prevail"—the most majestic compound fracture of fact which any of woman born has yet achieved. For the history of our race, and each individual's experience, are sown thick with evidence that a truth is not hard to kill and that a lie told well is immortal. There in Boston is a monument of the man who discovered anaesthesia;[1] many people are aware, in these latter days, that that man didn't discover it at all, but stole the discovery from another man. Is this truth mighty, and will it prevail? Ah no, my hearers, the monument is made of hardy material, but the lie it tells will outlast it a million years. An awkward, feeble, leaky lie is a thing which you ought to make it your unceasing study to avoid; such a lie as that has no more real permanence than an average truth. Why, you might as well tell the truth at once and be done with it. A feeble, stupid, preposterous lie will not live two years—except it be a slander upon somebody. It is indestructible, then, of course, but that is no merit of yours. A final word: begin your practice of this gracious and beautiful art early—begin now. If I had begun earlier, I could have learned how.

Never handle firearms carelessly. The sorrow and suffering that have been caused through the innocent but heedless handling of firearms by the young! Only four days ago, right in the next farm house to the one where I am spending the summer, a grandmother, old and grey and sweet, one of the loveliest spirits in the land, was sitting at her work, when her young grandson crept in and got down an old, battered, rusty gun which had not been touched for many years and was supposed not to be loaded, and pointed it at her, laughing and threatening to shoot. In her fright she ran screaming and pleading toward the door on the other side of the room; but as she passed him he placed the gun almost against her very breast and pulled the trigger! He had supposed it was not loaded. And he was right—it wasn't. So there wasn't any harm done. It is the only case of that kind I ever heard of. Therefore, just the same, don't you meddle with old unloaded firearms; they are the most deadly and unerring things that have ever been created by man. You don't have to take any pains at all with them; you don't have to have a rest, you don't have to have any sights on the gun, you don't have to take aim, even. No, you just pick out a relative and bang away, and you are sure to get him. A youth who can't hit a cathedral at thirty yards with a Gatling gun[2] in three quarters of an hour, can take up an old empty musket and bag his grandmother every time, at a hundred. Think what Waterloo would have been if one of the armies had been boys armed with old muskets supposed not to be loaded, and the other army had been composed of their female relations. The very thought of it makes one shudder.

---

1   *monument ... anaesthesia* Monument commemorating the work of Dr. William Thomas Green Morton (1815–68), who was the first to publicly demonstrate the use of ether as an anaesthetic. His claim to be the sole discoverer of ether's anaesthetic effects was disputed by several people.

2   *Gatling gun* Early machine gun invented in the 1860s and used by the American military.

There are many sorts of books; but good ones are the sort for the young to read. Remember that. They are a great, an inestimable, an unspeakable means of improvement. Therefore be careful in your selection, my young friends; be very careful; confine yourselves exclusively to Robertson's Sermons, Baxter's *Saint's Rest*,[1] *The Innocents Abroad*, and works of that kind.

But I have said enough. I hope you will treasure up the instructions which I have given you, and make them a guide to your feet and a light to your understanding. Build your character thoughtfully and painstaking upon these precepts, and by and by, when you have got it built, you will be surprised and gratified to see how nicely and sharply it resembles everybody else's.

—(1882)

---

1   *Robertson's Sermons* Sermons by Anglican minister F.W. Robertson (1816–53), which were published in the decade after his death and were widely read and respected; *Baxter's Saint's Rest* Richard Baxter's devotional work *The Saint's Everlasting Rest* (1650), considered a spiritual classic.

Virginia Woolf
1882–1941

As a writer of daring and ambitious novels; a publisher of avant-garde work by figures such as T.S. Eliot and Katherine Mansfield; and a founding member of the Bloomsbury Group, a circle of brilliant English artists and intellectuals, Virginia Woolf was at the forefront of literary modernism and its revolt against traditional forms and styles. Today, she is admired and studied primarily as the author of such masterpieces as *Mrs Dalloway* (1925), *To the Lighthouse* (1927), and *The Waves* (1931), novels that attempt to capture the rhythms of consciousness by rendering the subjective interplay of perception, recollection, emotion, and understanding. But in her own lifetime Woolf was just as well known for her non-fiction, a vast body of journalism, criticism, and essays in which she draws on "the democratic art of prose" (in her own words) to communicate with a broader readership.

Two of Woolf's longer non-fiction works, *A Room of One's Own* (1929) and *Three Guineas* (1938), are now acknowledged as ground-breaking feminist studies of the social, psychological, and political effects of patriarchy. But many critics have tended to treat Woolf's essays as incidental works, interesting only insofar as they illuminate her fictional theory and practice. Woolf herself distinguished between professional and creative writing—the one a means to an income, the other part of a broader artistic project. The essays tend to be more formally conventional than the novels, but many of them are nonetheless remarkable for their expression of personality and their open engagement with ideas. Amiable and urbane, more exploratory than authoritative, they wander from topic to topic, full of idiosyncratic asides and digressions. Through her engagingly forthright tone Woolf often achieves a remarkable intimacy with the reader. She considered the possibility for creating such intimacy to be a chief virtue of the form: as she observed, a good essay "must draw its curtain round us, but it must be a curtain that shuts us in, not out."

The Death of the Moth

Moths that fly by day are not properly to be called moths; they do not excite that pleasant sense of dark autumn nights and ivy-blossom which the commonest yellow-underwing asleep in the shadow of the curtain never fails to rouse in us. They are hybrid creatures, neither gay like butterflies nor sombre like their own species. Nevertheless the present specimen, with his narrow hay-coloured wings, fringed with a tassel of the same colour, seemed to be content with life. It was a pleasant morning, mid–September, mild, benignant,

yet with a keener breath than that of the summer months. The plough was already scoring the field opposite the window, and where the share[1] had been, the earth was pressed flat and gleamed with moisture. Such vigour came rolling in from the fields and the down beyond that it was difficult to keep the eyes strictly turned upon the book. The rooks too were keeping one of their annual festivities; soaring round the tree tops until it looked as if a vast net with thousands of black knots in it had been cast up into the air; which, after a few moments sank slowly down upon the trees until every twig seemed to have a knot at the end of it. Then, suddenly, the net would be thrown into the air again in a wider circle this time, with the utmost clamour and vociferation, as though to be thrown into the air and settle slowly down upon the tree tops were a tremendously exciting experience.

The same energy which inspired the rooks, the ploughmen, the horses, and even, it seemed, the lean bare-backed downs, sent the moth fluttering from side to side of his square of the window-pane. One could not help watching him. One was, indeed, conscious of a queer feeling of pity for him. The possibilities of pleasure seemed that morning so enormous and so various that to have only a moth's part in life, and a day moth's at that, appeared a hard fate, and his zest in enjoying his meagre opportunities to the full, pathetic. He flew vigorously to one corner of his compartment, and, after waiting there a second, flew across to the other. What remained for him but to fly to a third corner and then to a fourth? That was all he could do, in spite of the size of the downs, the width of the sky, the far-off smoke of houses, and the romantic voice, now and then, of a steamer out at sea. What he could do he did. Watching him, it seemed as if a fibre, very thin but pure, of the enormous energy of the world had been thrust into his frail and diminutive body. As often as he crossed the pane, I could fancy that a thread of vital light became visible. He was little or nothing but life.

Yet, because he was so small, and so simple a form of the energy that was rolling in at the open window and driving its way through so many narrow and intricate corridors in my own brain and in those of other human beings, there was something marvellous as well as pathetic about him. It was as if someone had taken a tiny bead of pure life and decking it as lightly as possible with down and feathers, had set it dancing and zig-zagging to show us the true nature of life. Thus displayed one could not get over the strangeness of it. One is apt to forget all about life, seeing it humped and bossed and garnished and cumbered so that it has to move with the greatest circumspection and dignity. Again, the thought of all that life might have been had he been born in any other shape caused one to view his simple activities with a kind of pity.

---

1   *share* Blade of a plough.

After a time, tired by his dancing apparently, he settled on the window ledge in the sun, and, the queer spectacle being at an end, I forgot about him. Then, looking up, my eye was caught by him. He was trying to resume his dancing, but seemed either so stiff or so awkward that he could only flutter to the bottom of the window-pane; and when he tried to fly across it he failed. Being intent on other matters I watched these futile attempts for a time without thinking, unconsciously waiting for him to resume his flight, as one waits for a machine, that has stopped momentarily, to start again without considering the reason of its failure. After perhaps a seventh attempt he slipped from the wooden ledge and fell, fluttering his wings, on to his back on the window sill. The helplessness of his attitude roused me. It flashed upon me that he was in difficulties; he could no longer raise himself; his legs struggled vainly. But, as I stretched out a pencil, meaning to help him to right himself, it came over me that the failure and awkwardness were the approach of death. I laid the pencil down again.

The legs agitated themselves once more. I looked as if for the enemy against which he struggled. I looked out of doors. What had happened there? Presumably it was midday, and work in the fields had stopped. Stillness and quiet had replaced the previous animation. The birds had taken themselves off to feed in the brooks. The horses stood still. Yet the power was there all the same, massed outside indifferent, impersonal, not attending to anything in particular. Somehow it was opposed to the little hay-coloured moth. It was useless to try to do anything. One could only watch the extraordinary efforts made by those tiny legs against an oncoming doom which could, had it chosen, have submerged an entire city, not merely a city, but masses of human beings; nothing, I knew, had any chance against death. Nevertheless after a pause of exhaustion the legs fluttered again. It was superb this last protest, and so frantic that he succeeded at last in righting himself. One's sympathies, of course, were all on the side of life. Also, when there was nobody to care or to know, this gigantic effort on the part of an insignificant little moth, against a power of such magnitude, to retain what no one else valued or desired to keep, moved one strangely. Again, somehow, one saw life, a pure bead. I lifted the pencil again, useless though I knew it to be. But even as I did so, the unmistakable tokens of death showed themselves. The body relaxed, and instantly grew stiff. The struggle was over. The insignificant little creature now knew death. As I looked at the dead moth, this minute wayside triumph of so great a force over so mean an antagonist filled me with wonder. Just as life had been strange a few minutes before, so death was now as strange. The moth having righted himself now lay most decently and uncomplainingly composed. O yes, he seemed to say, death is stronger than I am.

—1942

Zora Neale Hurston
1891–1960

Today critics often speak of the resurrection of Zora Neale Hurston. Although among the most prolific African American writers of her generation, she spent her latter years in obscurity, earning a paltry and irregular subsistence as a maid, supply teacher, and sometime journalist. When she died in a county welfare home in Florida, she was buried in an unmarked grave, her achievements largely ignored or forgotten. It was not until 1975, when Alice Walker published her essay "In Search of Zora Neale Hurston," that the author of *Jonah's Gourd Vine* (1934) and *Their Eyes Were Watching God* (1937) was restored to her rightful place and recognized as "the intellectual and spiritual foremother of a generation of black women writers."

Many commentators on Hurston's novels, short stories, and pioneering studies of African folklore have been struck by what Walker describes as their exuberant "racial health—a sense of black people as complete, complex, *undiminished* human beings, a sense that is lacking in so much black writing and literature." Informed by the myths, rituals, and storytelling traditions that she documented in her anthropological work, Hurston's fiction celebrates black culture and the nuance and vitality of black vernacular speech. But her reluctance to use her art to "lecture on the race problem" or to give a politicized, sociological account of "the Negro" alienated many other prominent authors and intellectuals of the Harlem Renaissance. In a rancorous review of *Their Eyes Were Watching God*, Richard Wright accused Hurston of perpetuating a degrading minstrel tradition, dismissing her masterpiece as an exercise in "facile sensuality" that "carries no theme, no message, no thought."

Ever an individualist, Hurston refused to write resentful novels of social protest in which "black lives are only defensive reactions to white actions." As she declared in her essay "How It Feels to Be Coloured Me" (1928), "I do not belong to that sobbing school of Negrohood who hold that nature somehow has given them a lowdown dirty deal." Hurston's position was controversial, particularly in the era of Jim Crow segregation laws, but she sought after her own fashion to overcome what W.E.B. Du Bois called "the problem of the colour line" by opening up the souls of black men and women so as to reveal their common humanity and individual strength.

How It Feels to Be Coloured Me

I am coloured but I offer nothing in the way of extenuating circumstances except the fact that I am the only Negro in the United States whose grandfather on the mother's side was *not* an Indian chief.[1]

I remember the very day that I became coloured. Up to my thirteenth year I lived in the little Negro town of Eatonville, Florida. It is exclusively a coloured town. The only white people I knew passed through the town going to or coming from Orlando. The native whites rode dusty horses, the Northern tourists chugged down the sandy village road in automobiles. The town knew the Southerners and never stopped cane chewing when they passed. But the Northerners were something else again. They were peered at cautiously from behind curtains by the timid. The more venturesome would come out on the porch to watch them go past and got just as much pleasure out of the tourists as the tourists got out of the village.

The front porch might seem a daring place for the rest of the town, but it was a gallery[2] seat for me. My favourite place was atop the gate-post. Proscenium box for a born first-nighter.[3] Not only did I enjoy the show, but I didn't mind the actors knowing that I liked it. I usually spoke to them in passing. I'd wave at them and when they returned my salute, I would say something like this: "Howdy-do-well-I-thank-you-where-you-goin'?" Usually the automobile or the horse paused at this, and after a queer exchange of compliments, I would probably "go a piece of the way" with them, as we say in farthest Florida. If one of my family happened to come to the front in time to see me, of course negotiations would be rudely broken off. But even so, it is clear that I was the first "welcome-to-our-state" Floridian, and I hope the Miami Chamber of Commerce will please take notice.

During this period, white people differed from coloured to me only in that they rode through town and never lived there. They liked to hear me "speak pieces" and sing and wanted to see me dance the parse-me-la, and gave me generously of their small silver for doing these things, which seemed strange to me for I wanted to do them so much that I needed bribing to stop. Only they didn't know it. The coloured people gave no dimes. They deplored any joyful tendencies in me, but I was their Zora nevertheless. I belonged to them, to the nearby hotels, to the county—everybody's Zora.

---

1   *I am ... Indian chief* An improbably high number of African Americans claimed to have Native American heritage, which was prestigious in African American communities at this time.

2   *gallery* Theatre seating area situated in an elevated balcony.

3   *Proscenium box* Theatre seating area near the proscenium, the frame of the stage; *first-nighter* Person who frequently appears in the audience of opening night performances.

But changes came in the family when I was thirteen, and I was sent to school in Jacksonville. I left Eatonville, the town of the oleanders, as Zora. When I disembarked from the river-boat at Jacksonville, she was no more. It seemed that I had suffered a sea change. I was not Zora of Orange County any more, I was now a little coloured girl. I found it out in certain ways. In my heart as well as in the mirror, I became a fast[1] brown—warranted not to rub nor run.

But I am not tragically coloured. There is no great sorrow dammed up in my soul, nor lurking behind my eyes. I do not mind at all. I do not belong to the sobbing school of Negrohood who hold that nature somehow has given them a lowdown dirty deal and whose feelings are all hurt about it. Even in the helter-skelter skirmish that is my life, I have seen that the world is to the strong regardless of a little pigmentation more or less. No, I do not weep at the world—I am too busy sharpening my oyster knife.

Someone is always at my elbow reminding me that I am the granddaughter of slaves. It fails to register depression with me. Slavery is sixty years in the past.[2] The operation was successful and the patient is doing well, thank you. The terrible struggle that made me an American out of a potential slave said "On the line!" The Reconstruction[3] said "Get set!"; and the generation before said "Go!" I am off to a flying start and I must not halt in the stretch to look behind and weep. Slavery is the price I paid for civilization, and the choice was not with me. It is a bully[4] adventure and worth all that I have paid through my ancestors for it. No one on earth ever had a greater chance for glory. The world to be won and nothing to be lost. It is thrilling to think—to know that for any act of mine, I shall get twice as much praise or twice as much blame. It is quite exciting to hold the centre of the national stage, with the spectators not knowing whether to laugh or to weep.

The position of my white neighbour is much more difficult. No brown spectre pulls up a chair beside me when I sit down to eat. No dark ghost thrusts its leg against mine in bed. The game of keeping what one has is never so exciting as the game of getting.

---

1   *fast* Adjective applied to dyes that will not run or change colour.
2   *Slavery is ... the past* In 1863, the Emancipation Proclamation legally ended slavery in America.
3   *Reconstruction* Period of recovery (1865–77) after the American Civil War. During Reconstruction, the Southern states adjusted to an economy without legal slavery and rebuilt infrastructure that had been damaged by the war.
4   *bully* Merry, splendid.

I do not always feel coloured. Even now I often achieve the unconscious Zora of Eatonville before the Hegira.[1] I feel most coloured when I am thrown against a sharp white background.

For instance at Barnard.[2] "Beside the waters of the Hudson"[3] I feel my race. Among the thousand white persons, I am a dark rock surged upon, and overswept, but through it all, I remain myself. When covered by the waters, I am; and the ebb but reveals me again.

Sometimes it is the other way around. A white person is set down in our midst, but the contrast is just as sharp for me. For instance, when I sit in the drafty basement that is The New World Cabaret with a white person, my colour comes. We enter chatting about any little nothing that we have in common and are seated by the jazz waiters. In the abrupt way that jazz orchestras have, this one plunges into a number. It loses no time in circumlocutions, but gets right down to business. It constricts the thorax and splits the heart with its tempo and narcotic harmonies. This orchestra grows rambunctious, rears on its hind legs and attacks the tonal veil with primitive fury, rending it, clawing it until it breaks through to the jungle beyond. I follow those heathen—follow them exultingly. I dance wildly inside myself; I yell within, I whoop; I shake my assegai[4] above my head, I hurl it true to the mark *yeeeeooww*! I am in the jungle and living in the jungle way. My face is painted red and yellow and my body is painted blue. My pulse is throbbing like a war drum. I want to slaughter something—give pain, give death to what, I do not know. But the piece ends. The men of the orchestra wipe their lips and rest their fingers. I creep back slowly to the veneer we call civilization with the last tone and find the white friend sitting motionless in his seat smoking calmly.

"Good music they have here," he remarks, drumming the table with his fingertips.

Music. The great blobs of purple and red emotion have not touched him. He has only heard what I felt. He is far away and I see him but dimly across the ocean and the continent that have fallen between us. He is so pale with his whiteness then and I am *so* coloured.

At certain times I have no race, I am *me*. When I set my hat at a certain angle and saunter down Seventh Avenue, Harlem City, feeling as snooty as the lions

---

1   *Hegira* I.e., journey; refers to Mohammed's journey from Mecca to Medina, which marks the beginning of the current era in the Islamic calendar.

2   *Barnard* Women's liberal arts college in New York City, affiliated with Columbia University.

3   *Beside ... Hudson* Barnard school song.

4   *assegai* Spear made of a tree of the same name, used by people of southern Africa.

in front of the Forty-Second Street Library, for instance. So far as my feelings are concerned, Peggy Hopkins Joyce on the Boule Mich[1] with her gorgeous raiment, stately carriage, knees knocking together in a most aristocratic manner, has nothing on me. The cosmic Zora emerges. I belong to no race nor time. I am the eternal feminine with its string of beads.

I have no separate feeling about being an American citizen and coloured. I am merely a fragment of the Great Soul that surges within the boundaries. My country, right or wrong.

Sometimes, I feel discriminated against, but it does not make me angry. It merely astonishes me. How *can* any deny themselves the pleasure of my company? It's beyond me.

But in the main, I feel like a brown bag of miscellany propped against a wall. Against a wall in company with other bags, white, red and yellow. Pour out the contents, and there is discovered a jumble of small things priceless and worthless. A first-water[2] diamond, an empty spool, bits of broken glass, lengths of string, a key to a door long since crumbled away, a rusty knife-blade, old shoes saved for a road that never was and never will be, a nail bent under the weight of things too heavy for any nail, a dried flower or two still a little fragrant. In your hand is the brown bag. On the ground before you is the jumble it held—so much like the jumble in the bags, could they be emptied, that all might be dumped in a single heap and the bags refilled without altering the content of any greatly. A bit of coloured glass more or less would not matter. Perhaps that is how the Great Stuffer of Bags filled them in the first place—who knows?

—1928

---

1   *Peggy Hopkins Joyce* White American actress (1893–1957) known for her extravagant lifestyle; *Boule Mich* Boulevard Saint-Michel, a major street in Paris.

2   *first-water* Best quality of diamond or other gem.

George Orwell

1903–1950

George Orwell is best known to modern readers for two works: the anti-Stalinist allegory *Animal Farm* (1945) and the dystopian nightmare *1984* (1949). It was with reference to these two novels that the word "Orwellian" entered the English language as a signifier for any oppressive, invasive, and manipulative practice that seems to threaten the freedom of a society. Orwell was also a successful and prolific writer of non-fiction: full-length works of political and social criticism (notably *The Road to Wigan Pier*, *Down and Out in Paris and London*, and *Homage to Catalonia*) as well as essays of a variety of sorts (memoir, literary criticism, political journalism). The imprint he left on English literary non-fiction may be even deeper than that which he left on English fiction; the scholar Leo Rockas has said that "Orwell's style is probably more admired and pointed to as a model than any other modern prose style, primarily for its no-nonsense approach."

Eric Arthur Blair, the man who would become famous as George Orwell, was born in the Indian municipality of Motihari to an English father employed in the Indian Civil Service. His mother had grown up in Burma, where her French father pursued his business interests. When he was one year old, his mother took him and his older sister to live in England; there, Orwell attended a number of boarding schools, including Eton, in preparation for a university career. His Eastern origins, however, exerted a strong influence on the young man, and in 1922 Orwell left England to begin service with the Indian Imperial Police in Burma.

Orwell's time in Burma would inform his art and politics for the rest of his life. Most directly, he would draw on his experiences in writing essays such as "Shooting an Elephant" (1936). Beyond that, the distaste he developed in Burma for the imperial project continued to inform Orwell's treatment of the themes of authority, oppression, and moral conscience—in the novels *Animal Farm* and *1984* as well as in his non-fiction.

Shooting an Elephant

In Moulmein, in Lower Burma, I was hated by large numbers of people—the only time in my life that I have been important enough for this to happen to me. I was sub-divisional police officer of the town, and in an aimless, petty kind of way anti-European feeling was very bitter. No one had the guts to raise a riot, but if a European woman went through the bazaars alone somebody would probably spit betel[1] juice over her dress. As a police officer I was an ob-

---

1   *betel* Leaf and nut mixture that is chewed as a stimulant, common in Southeast Asia.

vious target and was baited whenever it seemed safe to do so. When a nimble Burman tripped me up on the football field and the referee (another Burman) looked the other way, the crowd yelled with hideous laughter. This happened more than once. In the end the sneering yellow faces of young men that met me everywhere, the insults hooted after me when I was at a safe distance, got badly on my nerves. The young Buddhist priests were the worst of all. There were several thousands of them in the town and none of them seemed to have anything to do except stand on street corners and jeer at Europeans.

All this was perplexing and upsetting. For at that time I had already made up my mind that imperialism was an evil thing and the sooner I chucked up my job and got out of it the better. Theoretically—and secretly, of course—I was all for the Burmese and all against their oppressors, the British. As for the job I was doing, I hated it more bitterly than I can perhaps make clear. In a job like that you see the dirty work of Empire at close quarters. The wretched prisoners huddling in the stinking cages of the lock-ups, the grey, cowed faces of the long-term convicts, the scarred buttocks of the men who had been flogged with bamboos—all these oppressed me with an intolerable sense of guilt. But I could get nothing into perspective. I was young and ill-educated and I had had to think out my problems in the utter silence that is imposed on every Englishman in the East. I did not even know that the British Empire is dying, still less did I know that it is a great deal better than the younger empires that are going to supplant it. All I knew was that I was stuck between my hatred of the empire I served and my rage against the evil-spirited little beasts who tried to make my job impossible. With one part of my mind I thought of the British Raj as an unbreakable tyranny, as something clamped down, *in saecula saeculorum*,[1] upon the will of prostrate peoples; with another part I thought that the greatest joy in the world would be to drive a bayonet into a Buddhist priest's guts. Feelings like these are the normal by-products of imperialism; ask any Anglo-Indian official, if you can catch him off duty.

One day something happened which in a roundabout way was enlightening. It was a tiny incident in itself, but it gave me a better glimpse than I had had before of the real nature of imperialism—the real motives for which despotic governments act. Early one morning the sub-inspector at a police station the other end of the town rang me up on the phone and said that an elephant was ravaging the bazaar. Would I please come and do something about it? I did not know what I could do, but I wanted to see what was happening and I got on to a pony and started out. I took my rifle, an old .44 Winchester and much too small to kill an elephant, but I thought the noise might be useful *in*

---

1   *in saecula saeculorum* Latin: for centuries upon centuries; forever. This phrase appears frequently in the New Testament.

terrorem.[1] Various Burmans stopped me on the way and told me about the elephant's doings. It was not, of course, a wild elephant, but a tame one which had gone "must."[2] It had been chained up, as tame elephants always are when their attack of "must" is due, but on the previous night it had broken its chain and escaped. Its mahout,[3] the only person who could manage it when it was in that state, had set out in pursuit, but had taken the wrong direction and was now twelve hours' journey away, and in the morning the elephant had suddenly reappeared in the town. The Burmese population had no weapons and were quite helpless against it. It had already destroyed somebody's bamboo hut, killed a cow and raided some fruit-stalls and devoured the stock; also it had met the municipal rubbish van and, when the driver jumped out and took to his heels, had turned the van over and inflicted violences upon it.

The Burmese sub-inspector and some Indian constables were waiting for me in the quarter where the elephant had been seen. It was a very poor quarter, a labyrinth of squalid bamboo huts, thatched with palmleaf, winding all over a steep hillside. I remember that it was a cloudy, stuffy morning at the beginning of the rains. We began questioning the people as to where the elephant had gone and, as usual, failed to get any definite information. That is invariably the case in the East; a story always sounds clear enough at a distance, but the nearer you get to the scene of events the vaguer it becomes. Some of the people said that the elephant had gone in one direction, some said that he had gone in another, some professed not even to have heard of any elephant. I had almost made up my mind that the whole story was a pack of lies, when we heard yells a little distance away. There was a loud, scandalized cry of "Go away, child! Go away this instant!" and an old woman with a switch in her hand came round the corner of a hut, violently shooing away a crowd of naked children. Some more women followed, clicking their tongues and exclaiming; evidently there was something that the children ought not to have seen. I rounded the hut and saw a man's dead body sprawling in the mud. He was an Indian, a black Dravidian coolie,[4] almost naked, and he could not have been dead many minutes. The people said that the elephant had come suddenly upon him round the corner of the hut, caught him with its trunk, put its foot on his back and ground him into the earth. This was the rainy season and the ground was soft, and his face had scored a trench a foot deep and a couple of yards long. He was lying on his belly with arms crucified and head sharply twisted to one side. His face was coated with mud, the eyes wide open, the

---

1   *in terrorem* Legal term for a warning; literally, Latin phrase meaning "in fear or alarm."
2   *must* Condition characterized by aggressive behaviour brought on by a surge in testosterone.
3   *mahout* Elephant trainer or keeper.
4   *Dravidian coolie* I.e., southern Indian manual labourer.

teeth bared and grinning with an expression of unendurable agony. (Never tell me, by the way, that the dead look peaceful. Most of the corpses I have seen looked devilish.) The friction of the great beast's foot had stripped the skin from his back as neatly as one skins a rabbit. As soon as I saw the dead man I sent an orderly to a friend's house nearby to borrow an elephant rifle. I had already sent back the pony, not wanting it to go mad with fright and throw me if it smelt the elephant.

The orderly came back in a few minutes with a rifle and five cartridges, and meanwhile some Burmans had arrived and told us that the elephant was in the paddy fields below, only a few hundred yards away. As I started forward practically the whole population of the quarter flocked out of the houses and followed me. They had seen the rifle and were all shouting excitedly that I was going to shoot the elephant. They had not shown much interest in the elephant when he was merely ravaging their homes, but it was different now that he was going to be shot. It was a bit of fun to them, as it would be to an English crowd; besides they wanted the meat. It made me vaguely uneasy. I had no intention of shooting the elephant—I had merely sent for the rifle to defend myself if necessary—and it is always unnerving to have a crowd following you. I marched down the hill, looking and feeling a fool, with the rifle over my shoulder and an ever-growing army of people jostling at my heels. At the bottom, when you got away from the huts, there was a metalled road and beyond that a miry waste of paddy fields a thousand yards across, not yet ploughed but soggy from the first rains and dotted with coarse grass. The elephant was standing eight yards from the road, his left side towards us. He took not the slightest notice of the crowd's approach. He was tearing up bunches of grass, beating them against his knees to clean them and stuffing them into his mouth.

I had halted on the road. As soon as I saw the elephant I knew with perfect certainty that I ought not to shoot him. It is a serious matter to shoot a working elephant—it is comparable to destroying a huge and costly piece of machinery—and obviously one ought not to do it if it can possibly be avoided. And at that distance, peacefully eating, the elephant looked no more dangerous than a cow. I thought then and I think now that his attack of "must" was already passing off; in which case he would merely wander harmlessly about until the mahout came back and caught him. Moreover, I did not in the least want to shoot him. I decided that I would watch him for a little while to make sure that he did not turn savage again, and then go home.

But at that moment I glanced round at the crowd that had followed me. It was an immense crowd, two thousand at the least and growing every minute. It blocked the road for a long distance on either side. I looked at the sea of yellow faces above the garish clothes—faces all happy and excited over this bit of fun, all certain that the elephant was going to be shot. They were watching me as they would watch a conjurer about to perform a trick. They did not like me, but with the magical rifle in my hands I was momentarily worth watching. And suddenly I realized that I should have to shoot the elephant after all. The people expected it of me and I had got to do it; I could feel their two thousand wills pressing me forward, irresistibly. And it was at this moment, as I stood there with the rifle in my hands, that I first grasped the hollowness, the futility of the white man's dominion in the East. Here was I, the white man with his gun, standing in front of the unarmed native crowd—seemingly the leading actor of the piece; but in reality I was only an absurd puppet pushed to and fro by the will of those yellow faces behind. I perceived in this moment that when the white man turns tyrant it is his own freedom that he destroys. He becomes a sort of hollow, posing dummy, the conventionalized figure of a sahib.[1] For it is the condition of his rule that he shall spend his life in trying to impress the "natives," and so in every crisis he has got to do what the "natives" expect of him. He wears a mask, and his face grows to fit it. I had got to shoot the elephant. I had committed myself to doing it when I sent for the rifle. A sahib has got to act like a sahib; he has got to appear resolute, to know his own mind and do definite things. To come all that way, rifle in hand, with two thousand people marching at my heels, and then to trail feebly away, having done nothing—no, that was impossible. The crowd would laugh at me. And my whole life, every white man's life in the East, was one long struggle not to be laughed at.

But I did not want to shoot the elephant. I watched him beating his bunch of grass against his knees, with that preoccupied grandmotherly air that elephants have. It seemed to me that it would be murder to shoot him. At that age I was not squeamish about killing animals, but I had never shot an elephant and never wanted to. (Somehow it always seems worse to kill a *large* animal.) Besides, there was the beast's owner to be considered. Alive, the elephant was worth at least a hundred pounds; dead, he would only be worth the value of his tusks, five pounds, possibly. But I had got to act quickly. I turned to some experienced-looking Burmans who had been there when we arrived, and asked them how the elephant had been behaving. They all said the same thing: he took no notice of you if you left him alone, but he might charge if you went too close to him.

It was perfectly clear to me what I ought to do. I ought to walk up to within, say, twenty-five yards of the elephant and test his behaviour. If he charged, I could shoot; if he took no notice of me, it would be safe to leave

---

1   *sahib* I.e., colonial Englishman; this title of respect was used to address European men in colonial India.

him until the mahout came back. But also I knew that I was going to do no such thing. I was a poor shot with a rifle and the ground was soft mud into which one would sink at every step. If the elephant charged and I missed him, I should have about as much chance as a toad under a steam-roller. But even then I was not thinking particularly of my own skin, only of the watchful yellow faces behind. For at that moment, with the crowd watching me, I was not afraid in the ordinary sense, as I would have been if I had been alone. A white man mustn't be frightened in front of "natives"; and so, in general, he isn't frightened. The sole thought in my mind was that if anything went wrong those two thousand Burmans would see me pursued, caught, trampled on and reduced to a grinning corpse like that Indian up the hill. And if that happened it was quite probable that some of them would laugh. That would never do.

There was only one alternative. I shoved the cartridges into the magazine and lay down on the road to get a better aim. The crowd grew very still, and a deep, low, happy sigh, as of people who see the theatre curtain go up at last, breathed from innumerable throats. They were going to have their bit of fun after all. The rifle was a beautiful German thing with cross-hair sights. I did not then know that in shooting an elephant one would shoot to cut an imaginary bar running from ear-hole to ear-hole. I ought, therefore, as the elephant was sideways on, to have aimed straight at his ear-hole, actually I aimed several inches in front of this, thinking the brain would be further forward.

When I pulled the trigger I did not hear the bang or feel the kick—one never does when a shot goes home—but I heard the devilish roar of glee that went up from the crowd. In that instant, in too short a time, one would have thought, even for the bullet to get there, a mysterious, terrible change had come over the elephant. He neither stirred nor fell, but every line of his body had altered. He looked suddenly stricken, shrunken, immensely old, as though the frightful impact of the bullet had paralysed him without knocking him down. At last, after what seemed a long time—it might have been five seconds, I dare say—he sagged flabbily to his knees. His mouth slobbered. An enormous senility seemed to have settled upon him. One could have imagined him thousands of years old. I fired again into the same spot. At the second shot he did not collapse but climbed with desperate slowness to his feet and stood weakly upright, with legs sagging and head drooping. I fired a third time. That was the shot that did for him. You could see the agony of it jolt his whole body and knock the last remnant of strength from his legs. But in falling he seemed for a moment to rise, for as his hind legs collapsed beneath him he seemed to tower upward like a huge rock toppling, his trunk reaching skyward like a tree. He trumpeted, for the first and only time. And then down he came, his belly towards me, with a crash that seemed to shake the ground even where I lay.

I got up. The Burmans were already racing past me across the mud. It was obvious that the elephant would never rise again, but he was not dead. He was breathing very rhythmically with long rattling gasps, his great mound of a side painfully rising and falling. His mouth was wide open—I could see far down into caverns of pale pink throat. I waited a long time for him to die, but his breathing did not weaken. Finally I fired my two remaining shots into the spot where I thought his heart must be. The thick blood welled out of him like red velvet, but still he did not die. His body did not even jerk when the shots hit him, the tortured breathing continued without a pause. He was dying, very slowly and in great agony, but in some world remote from me where not even a bullet could damage him further. I felt that I had got to put an end to that dreadful noise. It seemed dreadful to see the great beast lying there, powerless to move and yet powerless to die, and not even to be able to finish him. I sent back for my small rifle and poured shot after shot into his heart and down his throat. They seemed to make no impression. The tortured gasps continued as steadily as the ticking of a clock.

In the end I could not stand it any longer and went away. I heard later that it took him half an hour to die. Burmans were bringing dahs[1] and baskets even before I left, and I was told they had stripped his body almost to the bones by the afternoon.

Afterwards, of course, there were endless discussions about the shooting of the elephant. The owner was furious, but he was only an Indian and could do nothing. Besides, legally I had done the right thing, for a mad elephant has to be killed, like a mad dog, if its owner fails to control it. Among the Europeans opinion was divided. The older men said I was right, the younger men said it was a damn shame to shoot an elephant for killing a coolie, because an elephant was worth more than any damn Coringhee[2] coolie. And afterwards I was very glad that the coolie had been killed; it put me legally in the right and it gave me a sufficient pretext for shooting the elephant. I often wondered whether any of the others grasped that I had done it solely to avoid looking a fool.

—1936

---

1   *dahs* Short swords or knives.
2   *Coringhee* From Coringha, a town on the coast of India.

Roland Barthes

1915–1980

Although scholars continue to debate the nature of his achievement, Roland Barthes, French critic, theorist, and champion of the avant-garde, was undoubtedly among the most influential intellectuals of the twentieth century. A pioneer in the field of semiology (the science of signs), and a trenchant critic of bourgeois culture and of the attitudes and values implicit in its icons, institutions, and "myths," Barthes has himself become something of a cultural icon. He is also famous for proclaiming "the death of the author" as the sovereign authority over textual meaning. Barthes is a difficult writer with whom to come to grips; the range of his interests and his highly idiosyncratic prose seem to be continually shifting—as are the contours of his thought.

Barthes is best known for his work on structuralism, an intellectual movement that grew out of the application of the methods and principles of structural linguistics to analyses of cultural phenomena, as a means of uncovering the system of codes and conventions whereby those phenomena are understood. He was also keenly interested in what he called "unlearning," the study of what is forgotten or taken for granted. By unmasking that which goes without saying, Barthes aims to reveal how the seemingly natural, self-evident meanings that circulate within a culture are in fact cultural products that support ideologies and serve particular social interests. We see this at play in *Mythologies* (1957), where Barthes brings his analytical powers to bear on a diverse host of subjects—wrestling, film, photography, wine, even children's toys—in an effort to expose the ideologically loaded secondary messages they emit.

Barthes is not without his detractors: skeptics have dismissed him as a dilettante whose convoluted theoretical pretensions ultimately lead to an intellectual dead end. But, as a "public experimenter" who took up and tested novel ideas and methods, Barthes opened new frontiers of critical study, challenging and transforming conventional views of authorship, realism, representation, the reading process, and the relationship between text and history.

The World of Wrestling

The grandiloquent truth of gestures on life's great occasions.[1]
—BAUDELAIRE

The virtue of all-in wrestling is that it is the spectacle of excess. Here we find a grandiloquence which must have been that of the ancient theatres. And in fact wrestling is an open-air spectacle, for what makes the circus[2] or the arena what they are is not the sky (a romantic value suited rather to fashionable occasions), it is the drenching and vertical quality of the flood of light. Even hidden in the most squalid Parisian halls, wrestling partakes of the nature of the great solar spectacles, Greek drama[3] and bull-fights: in both, a light without shadow generates an emotion without reserve.

There are people who think that wrestling is an ignoble sport. Wrestling is not a sport, it is a spectacle, and it is no more ignoble to attend a wrestled performance of Suffering than a performance of the sorrows of Arnolphe or Andromaque.[4] Of course, there exists a false wrestling, in which the participants unnecessarily go to great lengths to make a show of a fair fight; this is of no interest. True wrestling, wrongly called amateur wrestling, is performed in second-rate halls, where the public spontaneously attunes itself to the spectacular nature of the contest, like the audience at a suburban cinema. Then these same people wax indignant because wrestling is a stage-managed sport (which ought, by the way, to mitigate its ignominy). The public is completely uninterested in knowing whether the contest is rigged or not, and rightly so; it abandons itself to the primary virtue of the spectacle, which is to abolish all motives and all consequences: what matters is not what it thinks but what it sees.

This public knows very well the distinction between wrestling and boxing; it knows that boxing is ... based on a demonstration of excellence. One can bet on the outcome of a boxing-match: with wrestling, it would make no sense. A boxing-match is a story which is constructed before the eyes of the spectator; in wrestling, on the contrary, it is each moment which is intelligible, not the passage of time. The spectator is not interested in the rise and fall of

---

1   *The grandiloquent ... great occasions* From Charles Baudelaire, *Curiosités Esthétiques* (1868); *grandiloquent* Showy, grandiosely expressive.

2   *circus* Ancient outdoor stadium.

3   *Greek drama* In Ancient Athens, tragedies and comedies were performed in large outdoor arenas as part of mass religious festivals.

4   *Arnolphe* Protagonist of *The School for Wives* (1662), a play by the greatly admired French writer Molière; *Andromaque* Title character of a 1667 tragedy by Jean Racine, another widely respected French playwright.

fortunes; he expects the transient image of certain passions. Wrestling therefore demands an immediate reading of the juxtaposed meanings, so that there is no need to connect them. The logical conclusion of the contest does not interest the wrestling-fan, while on the contrary a boxing-match always implies a science of the future. In other words, wrestling is a sum of spectacles, of which no single one is a function: each moment imposes the total knowledge of a passion which rises erect and alone, without ever extending to the crowning moment of a result.

Thus the function of the wrestler is not to win; it is to go exactly through the motions which are expected of him. It is said that judo contains a hidden symbolic aspect; even in the midst of efficiency, its gestures are measured, precise but restricted, drawn accurately but by a stroke without volume. Wrestling, on the contrary, offers excessive gestures, exploited to the limit of their meaning. In judo, a man who is down is hardly down at all, he rolls over, he draws back, he eludes defeat, or, if the latter is obvious, he immediately disappears; in wrestling, a man who is down is exaggeratedly so, and completely fills the eyes of the spectators with the intolerable spectacle of his powerlessness.

This function of grandiloquence is indeed the same as that of ancient theatre, whose principle, language and props (masks and buskins[1]) concurred in the exaggeratedly visible explanation of a Necessity. The gesture of the vanquished wrestler signifying to the world a defeat which, far from disguising, he emphasizes and holds like a pause in music, corresponds to the mask of antiquity meant to signify the tragic mode of the spectacle. In wrestling, as on the stage in antiquity, one is not ashamed of one's suffering, one knows how to cry, one has a liking for tears.

Each sign[2] in wrestling is therefore endowed with an absolute clarity, since one must always understand everything on the spot. As soon as the adversaries are in the ring, the public is overwhelmed with the obviousness of the roles. As in the theatre, each physical type expresses to excess the part which has been assigned to the contestant. Thauvin, a fifty-year-old with an obese and sagging body, whose type of asexual hideousness always inspires feminine nicknames, displays in his flesh the characters of baseness, for his part is to represent what, in the classical concept of the *salaud*,[3] the "bastard" (the key-concept of any wrestling match), appears as organically repugnant. The nausea voluntarily provoked by Thauvin shows therefore a very extended use of signs: not only is ugliness used here in order to signify baseness, but in addition ugliness is wholly gathered into a particularly repulsive quality of matter: the pallid col-

---

1   *masks and buskins* The costumes for Greek tragic actors evolved to include highly stylized masks and boots called buskins, which had raised soles to make the actors appear taller.
2   *sign* Here, any unit that communicates meaning, such as a word, gesture, or image.
3   *salaud* French slang: bastard, someone despicably immoral and hypocritical.

lapse of dead flesh (the public calls Thauvin *la barbaque*, "stinking meat"), so that the passionate condemnation of the crowd no longer stems from its judgment, but instead from the very depth of its humours. It will thereafter let itself be frenetically embroiled in an idea of Thauvin which will conform entirely with this physical origin: his actions will perfectly correspond to the essential viscosity of his personage.

It is therefore in the body of the wrestler that we find the first key to the contest. I know from the start that all of Thauvin's actions, his treacheries, cruelties and acts of cowardice, will not fail to measure up to the first image of ignobility he gave me; I can trust him to carry out intelligently and to the last detail all the gestures of a kind of amorphous baseness, and thus fill to the brim the image of the most repugnant bastard there is: the bastard-octopus.... Thauvin will never be anything but an ignoble traitor, Reinières (a tall blond fellow with a limp body and unkempt hair) the moving image of passivity, Mazaud (short and arrogant like a cock) that of grotesque conceit, and Orsano (an effeminate teddy-boy first seen in a blue-and-pink dressing-gown) that, doubly humorous, of a vindictive *salope*,[1] or bitch....

The physique of the wrestlers therefore constitutes a basic sign, which like a seed contains the whole fight. But this seed proliferates, for it is at every turn during the fight, in each new situation, that the body of the wrestler casts to the public the magical entertainment of a temperament which finds its natural expression in a gesture. The different strata of meaning throw light on each other, and form the most intelligible of spectacles.... [A]bove the fundamental meaning of his body, the wrestler arranges comments which are episodic but always opportune, and constantly help the reading of the fight by means of gestures, attitudes and mimicry which make the intention utterly obvious. Sometimes the wrestler triumphs with a repulsive sneer while kneeling on the good sportsman; sometimes he gives the crowd a conceited smile which forebodes an early revenge; sometimes, pinned to the ground, he hits the floor ostentatiously to make evident to all the intolerable nature of his situation; and sometimes he erects a complicated set of signs meant to make the public understand that he legitimately personifies the ever-entertaining image of the grumbler, endlessly confabulating about his displeasure.

We are therefore dealing with a real Human Comedy, where the most socially-inspired nuances of passion (conceit, rightfulness, refined cruelty, a sense of "paying one's debts") always felicitously find the clearest sign which can receive them, express them and triumphantly carry them to the confines of the hall. It is obvious that at such a pitch, it no longer matters whether the passion is genuine or not. What the public wants is the image of passion, not pas-

---

1   *salope* French slang: bitch, slut; an insult typically directed at a woman.

sion itself. There is no more a problem of truth in wrestling than in the theatre. In both, what is expected is the intelligible representation of moral situations which are usually private. This emptying out of interiority to the benefit of its exterior signs, this exhaustion of the content by the form, is the very principle of triumphant classical art. Wrestling is an immediate pantomime, infinitely more efficient than the dramatic pantomime, for the wrestler's gesture needs no anecdote, no decor, in short no transference in order to appear true.

Each moment in wrestling is therefore like an algebra which instantaneously unveils the relationship between a cause and its represented effect. Wrestling fans certainly experience a kind of intellectual pleasure in *seeing* the moral mechanism function so perfectly. Some wrestlers, who are great comedians, entertain as much as a Molière character, because they succeed in imposing an immediate reading of their inner nature: Armand Mazaud, a wrestler of an arrogant and ridiculous character (as one says that Harpagon[1] is a character), always delights the audience by the mathematical rigour of his transcriptions, carrying the form of his gestures to the furthest reaches of their meaning, and giving to his manner of fighting a kind of vehemence and precision found in a great scholastic disputation,[2] in which what is at stake is at once the triumph of pride and the formal concern with truth.

What is thus displayed for the public is the great spectacle of Suffering, Defeat, and Justice. Wrestling presents man's suffering with all the amplification of tragic masks. The wrestler who suffers in a hold which is reputedly cruel (an arm-lock, a twisted leg) offers an excessive portrayal of Suffering; like a primitive Pietà,[3] he exhibits for all to see his face, exaggeratedly contorted by an intolerable affliction. It is obvious, of course, that in wrestling reserve would be out of place, since it is opposed to the voluntary ostentation of the spectacle, to this Exhibition of Suffering which is the very aim of the fight. This is why all the actions which produce suffering are particularly spectacular, like the gesture of a conjuror who holds out his cards clearly to the public. Suffering which appeared without intelligible cause would not be understood; a concealed action that was actually cruel would transgress the underwritten rules of wrestling and would have no more sociological efficacy than a mad or parasitic gesture. On the contrary suffering appears as inflicted with emphasis and conviction, for everyone must not only see that the man suffers, but also and above all understand why he suffers. What wrestlers call a hold, that is, any figure which allows one to immobilize the adversary indefinitely and to have him at one's mercy, has precisely the function of preparing in a conven-

---

1   *Harpagon* Stingy, old protagonist of Molière's comedy *The Miser* (1668).
2   *scholastic disputation* Formal philosophical argument of the sort conducted at medieval universities.
3   *Pietà* Work of art depicting the Virgin Mary holding Christ's dead body.

tional, therefore intelligible, fashion the spectacle of suffering, of methodically establishing the conditions of suffering. The inertia of the vanquished allows the (temporary) victor to settle in his cruelty and to convey to the public this terrifying slowness of the torturer who is certain about the outcome of his actions; to grind the face of one's powerless adversary or to scrape his spine with one's fist with a deep and regular movement, or at least to produce the superficial appearance of such gestures: wrestling is the only sport which gives such an externalized image of torture. But here again, only the image is involved in the game, and the spectator does not wish for the actual suffering of the contestant; he only enjoys the perfection of an iconography. It is not true that wrestling is a sadistic spectacle: it is only an intelligible spectacle.

There is another figure, more spectacular still than a hold; it is the forearm smash, this loud slap of the forearm, this embryonic punch with which one clouts the chest of one's adversary, and which is accompanied by a dull noise and the exaggerated sagging of a vanquished body. In the forearm smash, catastrophe is brought to the point of maximum obviousness, so much so that ultimately the gesture appears as no more than a symbol; this is going too far, this is transgressing the moral rules of wrestling, where all signs must be excessively clear, but must not let the intention of clarity be seen. The public then shouts "He's laying it on!," not because it regrets the absence of real suffering, but because it condemns artifice: as in the theatre, one fails to put the part across as much by an excess of sincerity as by an excess of formalism.

We have already seen to what extent wrestlers exploit the resources of a given physical style, developed and put to use in order to unfold before the eyes of the public a total image of Defeat. The flaccidity of tall white bodies which collapse with one blow or crash into the ropes with arms flailing, the inertia of massive wrestlers rebounding pitiably off all the elastic surfaces of the ring, nothing can signify more clearly and more passionately the exemplary abasement of the vanquished. Deprived of all resilience, the wrestler's flesh is no longer anything but an unspeakable heap spread out on the floor, where it solicits relentless reviling and jubilation. There is here a paroxysm of meaning in the style of antiquity, which can only recall the heavily underlined intentions in Roman triumphs. At other times, there is another ancient posture which appears in the coupling of the wrestlers, that of the suppliant who, at the mercy of his opponent, on bended knees, his arms raised above his head, is slowly brought down by the vertical pressure of the victor. In wrestling, unlike judo, Defeat is not a conventional sign, abandoned as soon as it is understood; it is not an outcome, but quite the contrary, it is a duration, a display, it takes up the ancient myths of public Suffering and Humiliation: the cross and the pillory. It is as if the wrestler is crucified in broad daylight and in the sight of all. I have heard it said of a wrestler stretched on the ground: "He is dead, little Jesus, there, on the cross," and these ironic words revealed the hidden roots of a spectacle which enacts the exact gestures of the most ancient purifications.

But what wrestling is above all meant to portray is a purely moral concept: that of justice. The idea of "paying" is essential to wrestling, and the crowd's "Give it to him" means above all else "Make him pay." This is therefore, needless to say, an immanent justice. The baser the action of the "bastard," the more delighted the public is by the blow which he justly receives in return. If the villain—who is of course a coward—takes refuge behind the ropes, claiming unfairly to have a right to do so by a brazen mimicry, he is inexorably pursued there and caught, and the crowd is jubilant at seeing the rules broken for the sake of a deserved punishment. Wrestlers know very well how to play up to the capacity for indignation of the public by presenting the very limit of the concept of Justice, this outermost zone of confrontation where it is enough to infringe the rules a little more to open the gates of a world without restraints. For a wrestling-fan, nothing is finer than the revengeful fury of a betrayed fighter who throws himself vehemently not on a successful opponent but on the smarting image of foul play. Naturally, it is the pattern of Justice which matters here, much more than its content: wrestling is above all a quantitative sequence of compensations (an eye for an eye, a tooth for a tooth). This explains why sudden changes of circumstances have in the eyes of wrestling habitués a sort of moral beauty: they enjoy them as they would enjoy an inspired episode in a novel, and the greater the contrast between the success of a move and the reversal of fortune, the nearer the good luck of a contestant to his downfall, the more satisfying the dramatic mime is felt to be. Justice is therefore the embodiment of a possible transgression; it is from the fact that there is a Law that the spectacle of the passions which infringe it derives its value.

It is therefore easy to understand why out of five wrestling-matches, only about one is fair. One must realize, let it be repeated, that "fairness" here is a role or a genre, as in the theatre: the rules do not at all constitute a real constraint; they are the conventional appearance of fairness. So that in actual fact a fair fight is nothing but an exaggeratedly polite one: the contestants confront each other with zeal, not rage; they can remain in control of their passions, they do not punish their beaten opponent relentlessly, they stop fighting as soon as they are ordered to do so, and congratulate each other at the end of a particularly arduous episode, during which, however, they have not ceased to be fair. One must of course understand here that all these polite actions are brought to the notice of the public by the most conventional gestures of fairness: shaking hands, raising the arms, ostensibly avoiding a fruitless hold which would detract from the perfection of the contest.

Conversely, foul play exists only in its excessive signs: administering a big kick to one's beaten opponent, taking refuge behind the ropes while ostensibly invoking a purely formal right, refusing to shake hands with one's opponent before or after the fight, taking advantage of the end of the round to rush treacherously at the adversary from behind, fouling him while the referee is not looking (a move which obviously only has any value or function because in fact half the audience can see it and get indignant about it). Since Evil is the natural climate of wrestling, a fair fight has chiefly the value of being an exception. It surprises the aficionado, who greets it when he sees it as an anachronism and a rather sentimental throwback to the sporting tradition ("Aren't they playing fair, those two"); he feels suddenly moved at the sight of the general kindness of the world, but would probably die of boredom and indifference if wrestlers did not quickly return to the orgy of evil which alone makes good wrestling.

Extrapolated, fair wrestling could lead only to boxing or judo, whereas true wrestling derives its originality from all the excesses which make it a spectacle and not a sport. The ending of a boxing-match or a judo-contest is abrupt, like the full-stop which closes a demonstration. The rhythm of wrestling is quite different, for its natural meaning is that of rhetorical amplification: the emotional magniloquence,[1] the repeated paroxysms, the exasperation of the retorts can only find their natural outcome in the most baroque confusion. Some fights, among the most successful kind, are crowned by a final charivari,[2] a sort of unrestrained fantasia where the rules, the laws of the genre, the referee's censuring and the limits of the ring are abolished, swept away by a triumphant disorder which overflows into the hall and carries off pell-mell wrestlers, seconds, referee and spectators....

What then is a "bastard" for this audience composed in part, we are told, of people who are themselves outside the rules of society? Essentially someone unstable, who accepts the rules only when they are useful to him and transgresses the formal continuity of attitudes. He is unpredictable, therefore asocial. He takes refuge behind the law when he considers that it is in his favour, and breaks it when he finds it useful to do so. Sometimes he rejects the formal boundaries of the ring and goes on hitting an adversary legally protected by the ropes, sometimes he reestablishes these boundaries and claims the protection of what he did not respect a few minutes earlier. This inconsistency, far more than treachery or cruelty, sends the audience beside itself with rage: offended not in its morality but in its logic, it considers the contradiction of arguments as the basest of crimes. The forbidden move becomes dirty only when it de-

---

1   *magniloquence* Excessive pomposity, usually in reference to speech or writing.
2   *charivari* Raucous procession of people making discordant noise by shouting, banging objects, blowing whistles, etc.

stroys a quantitative equilibrium and disturbs the rigorous reckoning of compensations; what is condemned by the audience is not at all the transgression of insipid official rules, it is the lack of revenge, the absence of a punishment. So that there is nothing more exciting for a crowd than the grandiloquent kick given to a vanquished "bastard"; the joy of punishing is at its climax when it is supported by a mathematical justification; contempt is then unrestrained. One is no longer dealing with a *salaud* but with a *salope*—the verbal gesture of the ultimate degradation.

Such a precise finality demands that wrestling should be exactly what the public expects of it. Wrestlers, who are very experienced, know perfectly how to direct the spontaneous episodes of the fight so as to make them conform to the image which the public has of the great legendary themes of its mythology. A wrestler can irritate or disgust, he never disappoints, for he always accomplishes completely, by a progressive solidification of signs, what the public expects of him. In wrestling, nothing exists except in the absolute, there is no symbol, no allusion, everything is presented exhaustively. Leaving nothing in the shade, each action discards all parasitic meanings and ceremonially offers to the public a pure and full signification, rounded like Nature. This grandiloquence is nothing but the popular and age-old image of the perfect intelligibility of reality. What is portrayed by wrestling is therefore an ideal understanding of things; it is the euphoria of men raised for a while above the constitutive ambiguity of everyday situations and placed before the panoramic view of a univocal Nature, in which signs at last correspond to causes, without obstacle, without evasion, without contradiction.

When the hero or the villain of the drama, the man who was seen a few minutes earlier possessed by moral rage, magnified into a sort of metaphysical sign, leaves the wrestling hall, impassive, anonymous, carrying a small suitcase and arm-in-arm with his wife, no one can doubt that wrestling holds that power of transmutation which is common to the Spectacle and to Religious Worship. In the ring, and even in the depths of their voluntary ignominy, wrestlers remain gods because they are, for a few moments, the key which opens Nature, the pure gesture which separates Good from Evil, and unveils the form of a Justice which is at last intelligible.

—1972

Richard Wagamese

1955–2017

In an interview with *The Globe and Mail*, Ojibwe novelist, memoirist, and journalist Richard Wagamese said, "I get my inspiration from the knowledge that there is someone out there in the world who is just like me—curious and desiring more and more knowledge of the world and her people." Wagamese's writing offers not only compelling testimony of the intergenerational trauma caused by colonization, but also powerful meditations on ways to heal those who have been wounded. He has been praised for the "pervasive humanity" his prose style brings to this project: his writing, critics have said, displays "a level of artistry so superb that the personal becomes eternal."

Wagamese was born in 1955 on the Wabaseemoong First Nation into a family haunted by their experiences in residential schools. "Each of the adults had suffered in an institution that tried to scrape the Indian out of their insides," he explained. "[T]hey came back to the bush raw, sore and aching." At the age of two, Wagamese was taken into custody by the Children's Aid Society. After going through three foster homes, he was adopted by a family of strict Presbyterians, who moved him to St. Catharines, Ontario. At age 16, Wagamese left his adoptive home and spent years living on the street. Finding refuge in a library, he received encouragement from the library staff and educated himself in literature, music, mathematics, and science. "The only thing I've taken is the open opportunity that lay between the open covers of a book," Wagamese noted. "I read and read, and by sheer volume alone, I found out what a good sentence was."

In 1979, Wagamese secured a journalist position with *The New Breed*, an Indigenous newspaper in Regina. He would later write as an Indigenous-affairs columnist for *The Calgary Herald*, for which he received a National Newspaper Award in 1991. He received immediate critical acclaim for his first novel, *The Keeper'n Me* (1994). He is perhaps best known for his 2012 novel *Indian Horse*, which was a finalist on the CBC program *Canada Reads*, although Wagamese believed his final novel, *Medicine Walk* (2014), to be his best; it has indeed received wide acclaim for its "sly humour, sharp, believable dialogue and superb storytelling."

Finding Father

In the dream I am running. There's a dim trail through the trees making the footing dangerous. Everywhere there are humped and snaking roots of trees and rocks broad across the back as bread loaves and tall ferns and saplings that whip across my face. But I'm moving as fast as I can. The oversized gumboots I wear make speed even more treacherous. They slap and clap against my shins

and flap around my foot at every stride. Still I run. There's a break in the trees and I can see the flash of white water from the rapids and I can hear the river's churning. From behind me I hear my pursuer. Heavy footfalls. Ravaged breath. I run hunched over trying to keep the gumboots on my feet fleeing for the safety of the river.

When I burst clear of the trees the sudden flare of light blinds me. But I sprint out onto the long, flat white peninsula of granite that pokes out into the river above the rapids. There are canoes there. I hope to jump into one and push it out into the current and down the chute of the rapids. I never get that chance.

Giant hands sweep me up. I'm spun in a wild circle. Large, strong arms enfold me. All I see is a whirl of long black hair like a curtain descending around me, falling over me, removing me from the world, the scent of wood smoke, bear grease and tanned hide, then deep laughter and the feel of a large palm at the back of my head. I'm laughing too as the gumboots fall from my feet. The world becomes the heat of the sun on my back and the feel of a big, warm heart beating against my tiny chest.

That dream is all I ever knew of my father.

I am Ojibway. My people occupy the large northern reaches of Ontario. We are bush people, river people, hunters, trappers and fishermen. I was born in a canvas army tent on a trap line. The first sounds I heard were an eagle's cry, the slap of a beaver's tail, the crackle of a fire and soft roll of Ojibway as my family talked and told stories around that fire. I was born to be one of them. But time and politics and history prevented that from happening.

I became one of the disappeared ones. I became one of the thousands of Aboriginal children across Canada swept up in the Sixties Scoop. This was an action by the government in conjunction with foster-care agencies to arbitrarily remove kids from their people. We were transplanted hundreds and thousands of miles away from our home territories. Some were even sent to different continents. We were routinely sold to outside foster-care agencies. I was one of those disenfranchised kids. I disappeared into non-native care before I was even two. I never made it home until I was twenty-four. Most of us never did.

My father's name was Stanley Raven. There were a number of men who adopted the name and role of father in my life when I was disappeared. None of them affected permanence. None of them fit the parameters of my dream. Stanley Raven was my one and only father and he died in a fall from a railway bridge the year before I made it home. There are few pictures of him. A bushman's life seldom includes photographs and all I learned of my father were stories my mother and elder sister told. He lives for me in the rough and tangle of the northern Ontario landscape. I hear his voice in the rush of rapids, in the pastoral stillness of a northern lake at sunset, in the rutting call of a moose and the haunting soliloquy of a lone wolf howling at a gibbous moon rising above the trees and ridges. Stanley Raven. In those four syllables lays a history I can never reclaim and a connection to this earth, to the territory of my people I can never fully forge—and in this my wound became geography.

The land itself haunted me. I couldn't walk the Winnipeg River without an all consuming tide of loss washing over me, could never stand on that railway bridge without scanning the rocks and trees for the dim path that might lead me to the camp he had set in the bush beyond it, could never hunt without the idea of him guiding me, teaching me, assuring me, could never watch the moon rise there without a wild keening rising from the depths of me.

So I set out to find him in the early fall of 1983.

"Where was the camp where I was born?" I asked my sister Jane.

"I don't think I could even find it," she said. "But it's across the bay from Minaki.[1] There's a long narrow cove with big birches at the end of it. It's somewhere back there." In a landscape of bush and rivers it was an inadequate description. "Who's taking you there?" she asked.

"Just me," I said. "Something I gotta do alone."

She looked at me searchingly. Then she nodded. "Picking up the trail," she said.

I nodded. She never asked me any questions after that. Instead she helped me fill a backpack with things I would need for a couple days in the bush and arranged for a family friend to loan me a boat motor for the trip. When I pushed off from the dock she stood there and watched and waved until I disappeared around a bend in the river.

Our family name, Wagamese, means crooked water. It's in reference to the Winnipeg River. It refers specifically to my great grandfather who worked a trap line through sixty miles of bush that ran along that river. It's my family's territory and my legacy even though we were all removed from it by the fall of 1983. But setting out alone on that river felt right to me and trailing a hand over the gunwale of the boat I felt a connection to its tea coloured depths. If history has a smell then the mineral scent of that river on my hand is mine. If time can be erased and geography can return us to the people we were born to be then the wash of that water across my face was my act of reclamation and redemption. All through that trip downriver, around the cascade of rapids, into the long, sleek, flat muscle of channels, around the hem of islands jutted with white pine and birch and thrusts of pink granite, I let it seep into me and found release in the sudden spray of heron from a tree, the sovereign stance

---

1   *Minaki* Community in northwestern Ontario.

of a moose knee deep in shallows eating lily pads, and the dark punctuation of a bear against the loose paragraph of the hills.

It took hours to get to Minaki. Then I turned south and west into a broad bay and began searching its far shore for the inlet my sister described. I found it just as evening was beginning to fall. There was just enough time to set up camp and light a fire before the thick dark blanket of night fell over everything. I sat up late. When the moon rose I walked to the shore and looked up at millions of stars. I stood in the presence of a deep and profound silence and did not feel the least bit lonely.

In the morning I found an old pit. I dragged a log over and sat on it. I had no idea if it marked the site I was looking for, had no idea if it was my father's hands that had built it. But in the dappled light of that small clearing I chose to believe he had. I chose to believe that he'd held me in that clearing, clasped me to his chest and cried tears of welcome then raised me up to the universe and spoke my name to it, introduced me to both it and the land around me in the language of my people, gave me both blessing and purpose right there in that small clearing so many years before. I sat there for a long time until the shifting light told me it was time to go.

I found my father on that journey. Found him in the shards of rock around an old fire. Found him in the scent of a river, in the ragged spire of granite cliffs, in the depths of the bush and in the image of a ragged white pine perched alone at the top of a cliff lurched leeward by persistent winds, standing alone against time and circumstance, proudly like a prodigal returned to the land that spawned him.

I still have the dream only now we run together into the light.

—2015

Scott McCloud
b. 1960

Scott McCloud is an American cartoonist and author best known for his pioneering work in the theorization of comics: as one critic has commented, "What Aristotle did" for Ancient Greek theatre, "McCloud has done for the neglected form of comics." Addressing a medium that was long dismissed as a childish distraction undeserving of critical analysis, McCloud has made a compelling case for regarding comics as serious works of art. In his seminal text *Understanding Comics* (1993), McCloud developed a sophisticated framework for examining the unique possibilities offered by the comic medium.

Growing up in Lexington, Massachusetts, McCloud began producing comic art in high school. "As soon as I started making my own comics," he recalled, "I began coming up with ideas for how comics worked." Unable to study comics in university, he majored in illustration, producing a portfolio that secured him a job at DC Comics, where he wrote for the *Superman Adventures* series as well as other DC projects.

McCloud defends the comic as a distinct medium of art with its own aesthetic criteria, "visual vocabulary," and methods for representing space and time. In *Understanding Comics*, he offers a tentative theoretical definition of the form, suggesting that comics should be broadly conceptualized as "juxtaposed pictorial and other images in deliberate sequence, intended to convey information and/or produce an aesthetic response in the reader." McCloud has since published other comics examining the medium, including *Reinventing Comics* (2000) and *Making Comics* (2006).

Throughout his career, McCloud has tested the boundaries of the comic medium and defied conventional wisdom about the "right" way to produce comics. In 1984, he created *Zot!*, a playful take on the superhero comic, which eschewed the violence and pessimism that was typical of mainstream comics at the time. Beginning in 1998, McCloud released a succession of "infinite canvas" comics, which took advantage of electronic technologies that have obviated the need to divide comics into pages.

McCloud has already left an enduring legacy as one of the first figures to acknowledge comics as generative objects of study. As one critic put it, "If you want to read ambitious comics and graphic novels, you have many choices, but if you want to learn how to read them, you probably have to start with Scott McCloud."

from *Understanding Comics*

THE ART FORM OF COMICS IS MANY CENTURIES OLD, BUT IT'S *PERCEIVED* AS A RECENT INVENTION AND SUFFERS THE CURSE OF *ALL* NEW MEDIA,

THE CURSE OF BEING JUDGED BY THE STANDARDS OF THE OLD.

EVER SINCE THE INVENTION OF THE WRITTEN WORD, NEW MEDIA HAVE BEEN *MISUNDERSTOOD.*

CAREFUL, JACOB! IF YOU KEEP DOING THIS, YOU'LL STOP USING YOUR *MEMORY!*

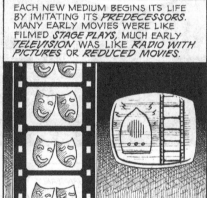

EACH NEW MEDIUM BEGINS ITS LIFE BY IMITATING ITS *PREDECESSORS.* MANY EARLY MOVIES WERE LIKE FILMED *STAGE PLAYS,* MUCH EARLY *TELEVISION* WAS LIKE *RADIO WITH PICTURES* OR *REDUCED MOVIES.*

FAR TOO MANY COMICS CREATORS HAVE NO HIGHER GOAL THAN TO MATCH THE ACHIEVEMENTS OF OTHER MEDIA, AND VIEW ANY CHANCE TO *WORK* IN OTHER MEDIA AS A *STEP UP.*

AND *AGAIN,* AS LONG AS WE VIEW COMICS AS A *GENRE* OF WRITING OR A *STYLE* OF GRAPHIC ART THIS ATTITUDE MAY *NEVER* DISAPPEAR.

WORDS AND PICTURES IN COMBINATION MAY NOT BE MY *DEFINITION* OF COMICS, BUT THE COMBINATION HAS HAD *TREMENDOUS INFLUENCE* ON ITS *GROWTH*.

com·ics (kom'iks) n. pl. ... form, used with a singular ... Juxtaposed pictori... ...er images in deliberate ... ...ence, intended to conve... ...on and/or to prod... response in the ... 2. Superheroes ... costumes, figh... villains who want ... ...he words in violent so... ...ruse...

A HUGE RANGE OF HUMAN EXPERIENCES CAN BE *PORTRAYED* IN COMICS THROUGH EITHER WORDS OR PICTURES.

AS A RESULT--AND DESPITE ITS MANY *OTHER* POTENTIAL USES -- COMICS HAVE BECOME *FIRMLY IDENTIFIED* WITH THE ART OF *STORYTELLING*.

AND *INDEED*, WORDS AND PICTURES HAVE *GREAT* POWERS TO TELL STORIES WHEN CREATORS FULLY EXPLOIT THEM *BOTH*.

DADA

BIOGRAPHY   HORROR

ROMANCE   SURREALISM

BLANK VERSE

EPIC POETRY

SOCIAL ALLEGORY

SEQUENTIAL ART

HISTORICAL FICTION

FOLK TALES

EROTICA

MYSTERY

ADAPTATIONS   RELIGIOUS TOPICS

STREAM OF CONSCIOUSNESS

SATIRE

AND SO FAR, WE'VE ONLY SEEN THE *TIP OF THE ICEBERG!*

AS CHILDREN, WE "SHOW AND TELL" *INTERCHANGEABLY*, WORDS AND IMAGES COMBINING TO TRANSMIT A *CONNECTED SERIES OF IDEAS*.

IT'S GOT ONE OF *THESE* THINGS.

THE DIFFERENT WAYS IN WHICH WORDS AND PICTURES CAN *COMBINE* IN COMICS IS VIRTUALLY *UNLIMITED*.

BUT LET'S TRY TO BREAK IT DOWN INTO SOME DISTINCT *CATEGORIES*.

FIRST, WE HAVE THE *WORD SPECIFIC* COMBINATIONS, WHERE PICTURES *ILLUSTRATE,* BUT DON'T SIGNIFICANTLY *ADD* TO A LARGELY *COMPLETE* TEXT.

WE STUMBLED BACK TO THE APARTMENT SHORTLY BEFORE DAWN, *VOMITING* EVERY 20 YARDS.

JUDY GAVE ME HER KEYS AND SMILED.

THE *UNITED STATES CONSTITUTION* WAS ADOPTED BY THE *SECOND CONTINENTAL CONGRESS* IN 1787 AND PUT INTO EFFECT IN 1789.

THEN THERE ARE *PICTURE SPECIFIC* COMBINATIONS WHERE WORDS DO LITTLE MORE THAN ADD A *SOUNDTRACK* TO A VISUALLY TOLD SEQUENCE.

HE DID IT!

MMM... MMM...

AND, OF COURSE, *DUO-SPECIFIC* PANELS IN WHICH BOTH WORDS AND PICTURES SEND ESSENTIALLY THE *SAME* MESSAGE.

GRIM-FACED, GEORGE LIFTED HIS LOLLYPOP.

BUT THE CAPTAIN'S MIGHTY BLOW *MISSES* ITS INTENDED TARGET!

BLAST! HE *DODGED* MY PUNCH AND I STRUCK THIS *BRICK WALL!*

HA.! I DODGED YOU

I FEEL SO *SAD!*

...THOUGHT AMY.

ANOTHER TYPE IS THE **ADDITIVE** COMBINATION WHERE WORDS *AMPLIFY* OR *ELABORATE* ON AN IMAGE OR *VICE VERSA.*

MY HEAD FEELS LIKE A *SMASHED PUMPKIN!*

HOW D'YA LIKE MY *NEW THREADS,* BABE?

IS THIS THE SAME *JUPITER* OF MY YOUTH?

IN **PARALLEL** COMBINATIONS, WORDS AND PICTURES SEEM TO FOLLOW VERY DIFFERENT COURSES--WITHOUT *INTERSECTING.*

"TALKED TO *BILL* YET?"

"*SALLY* DID. *WHY?*"

"THE *TEST RESULTS* CAME BACK. ALL *NEGATIVE.*"

"*REALLY?* THAT'S *GREAT!*"

WELL...

PEPPER.

CEREAL.

MILK.   BUTTER.

LIGHT BULBS.

STILL ANOTHER OPTION IS THE **MONTAGE** WHERE WORDS ARE TREATED AS INTEGRAL *PARTS* OF THE PICTURE.

CASH   PUBL
FLOWBOTTO
LINE
ANNUA
REPORT

HAPPY!

PERHAPS THE MOST *COMMON* TYPE OF WORD/PICTURE COMBINATION IS THE *INTER-DEPENDENT,* WHERE WORDS AND PICTURES GO *HAND IN HAND* TO CONVEY AN IDEA THAT NEITHER COULD CONVEY *ALONE.*

MEANWHILE...

DID ANYONE *SEE* YOU?

THIS IS ALL I NEED TO *STOP* HIM!

I ASK YOU, DOES THIS GUY LOOK LIKE A *C.E.O.* TO *YOU*??

"AND JUST *GUESS* WHO DROVE UP IN BOB'S TRUCK AN HOUR LATER!"

HEY, MARGE!

OH, MY GOD!

"AFTER COLLEGE, I PURSUED A CAREER IN *HIGH FINANCE.*"

HURRY UP, WILLYA?!

HE'S LYING.

UH-HUH.

INTERDEPENDENT COMBINATIONS AREN'T ALWAYS AN *EQUAL BALANCE* THOUGH AND MAY FALL *ANYWHERE* ON A SCALE BETWEEN TYPES ONE AND TWO.

GENERALLY SPEAKING, THE MORE IS SAID WITH *WORDS,* THE MORE THE PICTURES CAN BE FREED TO GO EXPLORING AND *VICE VERSA.*

$$\frac{P}{W}$$

$$\frac{W}{P}$$

IN COMICS AT ITS *BEST*, WORDS AND PICTURES ARE LIKE *PARTNERS* IN A *DANCE* AND EACH ONE TAKES TURNS *LEADING*.

WHEN *BOTH* PARTNERS TRY TO LEAD, THE COMPETITION CAN *SUBVERT* THE OVERALL GOALS...

YOW!

...THOUGH A LITTLE *PLAYFUL COMPETITION* CAN SOMETIMES PRODUCE *ENJOYABLE RESULTS*.

BUT WHEN THESE PARTNERS EACH *KNOW* THEIR ROLES--

--AND *SUPPORT* EACH OTHER'S *STRENGTHS*--

--COMICS CAN MATCH *ANY* OF THE ART FORMS IT DRAWS SO MUCH OF ITS STRENGTH FROM.

—1994

Philip Gourevitch
b. 1961

Philip Gourevitch is an American non-fiction writer and journalist. A staff writer for *The New Yorker* since 1997, he has travelled the world and reported on subjects such as genocide and war crimes, torture, terrorism, new political movements, and daily life in zones of conflict.

Born in Philadelphia and raised in central Connecticut, Gourevitch received a BA from Cornell University and an MFA from the Writing Program at Columbia. In addition to *The New Yorker*, he has published in *Granta*, *Harper's*, *The New York Times Magazine*, and *The New York Review of Books*. From 2005 to 2010, he served as editor of *The Paris Review*.

Gourevitch's third book, *Standard Operating Procedure* (2008), provides a "thorough, terrifying account" of a turning point in the Iraq War: the Abu Ghraib photographs of prisoner abuse. His second book, *Cold Case* (2001), reopens an investigation into a New York City double homicide that went unsolved for 30 years. But it was Gourevitch's first book that established him as one of the leading voices of his generation. *We Wish to Inform You That Tomorrow We Will Be Killed with Our Families* (1998) won many awards and has received wide recognition for shedding new light on the Rwandan genocide of 1994.

We Wish to Inform You contains visceral retellings of stories from individual Rwandan men and women. On six trips over nine months, Gourevitch gathered these stories on the ground. "Filled with empathy instead of cautious neutrality, and written in powerful muckraking prose, Gourevitch's book gives free rein to the anger—against both perpetrators and the international community—that others hold in check," wrote José E. Alvarez in *The American Journal of International Law*.

from *We Wish to Inform You That Tomorrow We Will Be Killed with Our Families*

In the Province of Kibungo, in eastern Rwanda, in the swamp- and pastureland near the Tanzanian border, there's a rocky hill called Nyarubuye with a church where many Tutsis[1] were slaughtered in mid-April of 1994. A year after the

---

1   *Tutsis* African ethnic group living primarily within Rwanda and neighbouring Burundi. In pre-colonial Rwanda, the Tutsis dominated the Hutu, an ethnic group constituting the majority of Rwanda's population. When the nation was controlled by European colonial powers—first Germany beginning in 1894, then Belgium after World War I—these governments reinforced the privilege of the Tutsis, exacerbating pre-existing ethnic tensions. The Hutu seized power from the Tutsis just before Rwanda achieved independence in

killing I went to Nyarubuye with two Canadian military officers. We flew in a United Nations helicopter, travelling low over the hills in the morning mists, with the banana trees like green starbursts dense over the slopes. The uncut grass blew back as we dropped into the centre of the parish schoolyard. A lone soldier materialized with his Kalashnikov, and shook our hands with stiff, shy formality. The Canadians presented the paperwork for our visit, and I stepped up into the open doorway of a classroom.

At least fifty mostly decomposed cadavers covered the floor, wadded in clothing, their belongings strewn about and smashed. Macheted[1] skulls had rolled here and there.

The dead looked like pictures of the dead. They did not smell. They did not buzz with flies. They had been killed thirteen months earlier, and they hadn't been moved. Skin stuck here and there over the bones, many of which lay scattered away from the bodies, dismembered by the killers, or by scavengers—birds, dogs, bugs. The more complete figures looked a lot like people, which they were once. A woman in a cloth wrap printed with flowers lay near the door. Her fleshless hip bones were high and her legs slightly spread, and a child's skeleton extended between them. Her torso was hollowed out. Her ribs and spinal column poked through the rotting cloth. Her head was tipped back and her mouth was open: a strange image—half agony, half repose.

I had never been among the dead before. What to do? Look? Yes. I wanted to see them, I suppose; I had come to see them—the dead had been left unburied at Nyarubuye for memorial purposes—and there they were, so intimately exposed. I didn't need to see them. I already knew, and believed, what had happened in Rwanda. Yet looking at the buildings and the bodies, and hearing the silence of the place, with the grand Italianate basilica standing there deserted, and beds of exquisite, decadent, death-fertilized flowers blooming over the corpses, it was still strangely unimaginable. I mean one still had to imagine it.

Those dead Rwandans will be with me forever, I expect. That was why I had felt compelled to come to Nyarubuye: to be stuck with them—not with their experience, but with the experience of looking at them. They had been killed there, and they were dead there. What else could you really see at first? The Bible bloated with rain lying on top of one corpse or, littered about, the little woven wreaths of thatch which Rwandan women wear as crowns to balance the enormous loads they carry on their heads, and the water gourds, and the Converse tennis sneaker stuck somehow in a pelvis.

1962, and ongoing conflict culminated in the Rwandan genocide, which lasted from April to mid-July in 1994. During the genocide, Hutu militias killed between 500,000 and 1 million Tutsis.

1   *Macheted* The machete—a large cleaver, intended for cutting jungle brush—was commonly used as a weapon during the genocide.

The soldier with the Kalashnikov—Sergeant Francis of the Rwandese Patriotic Army,[1] a Tutsi whose parents had fled to Uganda with him when he was a boy, after similar but less extensive massacres in the early 1960s, and who had fought his way home in 1994 and found it like this—said that the dead in this room were mostly women who had been raped before being murdered. Sergeant Francis had high, rolling girlish hips, and he walked and stood with his butt stuck out behind him, an oddly purposeful posture, tipped forward, driven. He was, at once, candid and briskly official. His English had the punctilious clip of military drill, and after he told me what I was looking at I looked instead at my feet. The rusty head of a hatchet lay beside them in the dirt.

A few weeks earlier, in Bukavu, Zaire, in the giant market of a refugee camp that was home to many Rwandan Hutu militiamen, I had watched a man butchering a cow with a machete. He was quite expert at his work, taking big precise strokes that made a sharp hacking noise. The rallying cry to the killers during the genocide was "Do your work!" And I saw that it *was* work, this butchery; hard work. It took many hacks—two, three, four, five hard hacks—to chop through the cow's leg. How many hacks to dismember a person?

Considering the enormity of the task, it is tempting to play with theories of collective madness, mob mania, a fever of hatred erupted into a mass crime of passion, and to imagine the blind orgy of the mob, with each member killing one or two people. But at Nyarubuye, and at thousands of other sites in this tiny country, on the same days of a few months in 1994, hundreds of thousands of Hutus had worked as killers in regular shifts. There was always the next victim, and the next. What sustained them, beyond the frenzy of the first attack, through the plain physical exhaustion and mess of it?

The pygmy in Gikongoro said that humanity is part of nature and that we must go against nature to get along and have peace. But mass violence, too, must be organized; it does not occur aimlessly. Even mobs and riots have a design, and great and sustained destruction requires great ambition. It must be conceived as the means toward achieving a new order, and although the idea behind that new order may be criminal and objectively very stupid, it must also be compellingly simple and at the same time absolute. The ideology of genocide is all of those things, and in Rwanda it went by the bald name of Hutu Power.[2] For those who set about systematically exterminating an entire

---

1   *Rwandese Patriotic Army* Armed forces of the Rwandese Patriotic Front (RPF), a leftist political party largely composed of Tutsis, which took power in Rwanda in the aftermath of the genocide. The genocide itself was triggered when Hutu extremists accused the RPF of assassinating Rwandan president Juvénal Habyarimana and Burundian president Cyprien Ntaryamira on 6 April 1994.

2   *Hutu Power* Ideology that asserted the superiority of Hutu people and the inferiority of the Tutsis.

people—even a fairly small and unresisting subpopulation of perhaps a million and a quarter men, women, and children, like the Tutsis in Rwanda—blood lust surely helps. But the engineers and perpetrators of a slaughter like the one just inside the door where I stood need not enjoy killing, and they may even find it unpleasant. What is required above all is that they want their victims dead. They have to want it so badly that they consider it a necessity.

So I still had much to imagine as I entered the classroom and stepped carefully between the remains. These dead and their killers had been neighbours, schoolmates, colleagues, sometimes friends, even in-laws. The dead had seen their killers training as militias in the weeks before the end, and it was well known that they were training to kill Tutsis; it was announced on the radio, it was in the newspapers, people spoke of it openly. The week before the massacre at Nyarubuye, the killing began in Rwanda's capital, Kigali. Hutus who opposed the Hutu Power ideology were publicly denounced as "accomplices" of the Tutsis and were among the first to be killed as the extermination got under way. In Nyarubuye, when Tutsis asked the Hutu Power mayor how they might be spared, he suggested that they seek sanctuary at the church. They did, and a few days later the mayor came to kill them. He came at the head of a pack of soldiers, policemen, militiamen, and villagers; he gave out arms and orders to complete the job well. No more was required of the mayor, but he was also said to have killed a few Tutsis himself.

The killers killed all day at Nyarubuye. At night they cut the Achilles tendons of survivors and went off to feast behind the church, roasting cattle looted from their victims in big fires, and drinking beer. (Bottled beer, banana beer—Rwandans may not drink more beer than other Africans, but they drink prodigious quantities of it around the clock.) And, in the morning, still drunk after whatever sleep they could find beneath the cries of their prey, the killers at Nyarubuye went back and killed again. Day after day, minute to minute, Tutsi by Tutsi: all across Rwanda, they worked like that. "It was a process," Sergeant Francis said. I can see that it happened, I can be told how, and after nearly three years of looking around Rwanda and listening to Rwandans, I can tell you how, and I will. But the horror of it—the idiocy, the waste, the sheer wrongness—remains uncircumscribable.

Like Leontius,[1] the young Athenian in Plato, I presume that you are reading this because you desire a closer look, and that you, too, are properly disturbed by your curiosity. Perhaps, in examining this extremity with me, you hope for some understanding, some insight, some flicker of self-knowledge—a

---

1   *Leontius* Character referred to in Plato's *Republic* (c. 380 BCE) who was reputedly unable to resist staring at a heap of dead bodies. Plato's Socrates tells the story of Leontius in order to illustrate the compulsiveness and irrationality of the appetitive—i.e., desiring—aspect of the human soul.

moral, or a lesson, or a clue about how to behave in this world: some such information. I don't discount the possibility, but when it comes to genocide, you already know right from wrong. The best reason I have come up with for looking closely into Rwanda's stories is that ignoring them makes me even more uncomfortable about existence and my place in it. The horror, as horror, interests me only insofar as a precise memory of the offence is necessary to understand its legacy.

The dead at Nyarubuye were, I'm afraid, beautiful. There was no getting around it. The skeleton is a beautiful thing. The randomness of the fallen forms, the strange tranquility of their rude exposure, the skull here, the arm bent in some uninterpretable gesture there—these things were beautiful, and their beauty only added to the affront of the place. I couldn't settle on any meaningful response: revulsion, alarm, sorrow, grief, shame, incomprehension, sure, but nothing truly meaningful. I just looked, and I took photographs, because I wondered whether I could really see what I was seeing while I saw it, and I wanted also an excuse to look a bit more closely.

We went on through the first room and out the far side. There was another room and another and another and another. They were all full of bodies, and more bodies were scattered in the grass and there were stray skulls in the grass, which was thick and wonderfully green. Standing outside, I heard a crunch. The old Canadian colonel stumbled in front of me, and I saw, though he did not notice, that his foot had rolled on a skull and broken it. For the first time at Nyarubuye my feelings focused, and what I felt was a small but keen anger at this man. Then I heard another crunch, and felt a vibration underfoot. I had stepped on one, too.

Rwanda is spectacular to behold. Throughout its centre, a winding succession of steep, tightly terraced slopes radiates out from small roadside settlements and solitary compounds. Gashes of red clay and black loam mark fresh hoe work; eucalyptus trees flash silver against brilliant green tea plantations; banana trees are everywhere. On the theme of hills, Rwanda produces countless variations: jagged rain forests, round-shouldered buttes, undulating moors, broad swells of savanna, volcanic peaks sharp as filed teeth. During the rainy season, the clouds are huge and low and fast, mists cling in highland hollows, lightning flickers through the nights, and by day the land is lustrous. After the rains, the skies lift, the terrain takes on a ragged look beneath the flat unvarying haze of the dry season, and in the savannas of the Akagera Park wildlife blackens the hills.

One day, when I was returning to Kigali from the south, the car mounted a rise between two winding valleys, the windshield filled with purple-bellied clouds, and I asked Joseph, the man who was giving me a ride, whether Rwandans realize what a beautiful country they have. "Beautiful?" he said. "You think so? After the things that happened here? The people aren't good. If the people were good, the country might be OK." Joseph told me that his brother and sister had been killed, and he made a soft hissing click with his tongue against his teeth. "The country is empty," he said. "Empty!"

It was not just the dead who were missing. The genocide had been brought to a halt by the Rwandese Patriotic Front, a rebel army led by Tutsi refugees from past persecutions, and as the RPF advanced through the country in the summer of 1994, some two million Hutus had fled into exile at the behest of the same leaders who had urged them to kill. Yet except in some rural areas in the south, where the desertion of Hutus had left nothing but bush to reclaim the fields around crumbling adobe houses, I, as a newcomer, could not see the emptiness that blinded Joseph to Rwanda's beauty. Yes, there were grenade-flattened buildings, burnt homesteads, shot-up facades, and mortar-pitted roads. But these were the ravages of war, not of genocide, and by the summer of 1995, most of the dead had been buried. Fifteen months earlier, Rwanda had been the most densely populated country in Africa. Now the work of the killers looked just as they had intended: invisible.

From time to time, mass graves were discovered and excavated, and the remains would be transferred to new, properly consecrated mass graves. Yet even the occasionally exposed bones, the conspicuous number of amputees and people with deforming scars, and the superabundance of packed orphanages could not be taken as evidence that what had happened to Rwanda was an attempt to eliminate a people. There were only people's stories.

"Every survivor wonders why he is alive," Abbé Modeste, a priest at the cathedral in Butare, Rwanda's second-largest city, told me. Abbé Modeste had hidden for weeks in his sacristy,[1] eating communion wafers, before moving under the desk in his study, and finally into the rafters at the home of some neighbouring nuns. The obvious explanation of his survival was that the RPF had come to the rescue. But the RPF didn't reach Butare till early July, and roughly seventy-five percent of the Tutsis in Rwanda had been killed by early May. In this regard, at least, the genocide had been entirely successful: to those who were targeted, it was not death but life that seemed an accident of fate.

"I had eighteen people killed at my house," said Etienne Niyonzima, a former businessman who had become a deputy in the National Assembly. "Everything was totally destroyed—a place of fifty-five metres by fifty metres. In my neighbourhood they killed six hundred and forty-seven people. They tortured them, too. You had to see how they killed them. They had the number

---

1   *sacristy* Room in a Christian church where priests and attendants prepare for mass or other religious services.

of everyone's house, and they went through with red paint and marked the homes of all the Tutsis and of the Hutu moderates. My wife was at a friend's, shot with two bullets. She is still alive, only"—he fell quiet for a moment— "she has no arms. The others with her were killed. The militia left her for dead. Her whole family of sixty-five in Gitarama were killed." Niyonzima was in hiding at the time. Only after he had been separated from his wife for three months did he learn that she and four of their children had survived. "Well," he said, "one son was cut in the head with a machete. I don't know where he went." His voice weakened, and caught. "He disappeared." Niyonzima clicked his tongue, and said, "But the others are still alive. Quite honestly, I don't understand at all how I was saved."

Laurent Nkongoli attributed his survival to "Providence,[1] and also good neighbours, an old woman who said, 'Run away, we don't want to see your corpse.'" Nkongoli, a lawyer, who had become the vice president of the National Assembly after the genocide, was a robust man, with a taste for double-breasted suit jackets and lively ties, and he moved, as he spoke, with a brisk determination. But before taking his neighbour's advice, and fleeing Kigali in late April of 1994, he said, "I had accepted death. At a certain moment this happens. One hopes not to die cruelly, but one expects to die anyway. Not death by machete, one hopes, but with a bullet. If you were willing to pay for it, you could often ask for a bullet. Death was more or less normal, a resignation. You lose the will to fight. There were four thousand Tutsis killed here at Kacyiru"—a neighbourhood of Kigali. "The soldiers brought them here, and told them to sit down because they were going to throw grenades. And they sat.

"Rwandan culture is a culture of fear," Nkongoli went on. "I remember what people said." He adopted a pipey voice, and his face took on a look of disgust: "'Just let us pray, then kill us,' or 'I don't want to die in the street, I want to die at home.'" He resumed his normal voice. "When you're that resigned and oppressed you're already dead. It shows the genocide was prepared for too long. I detest this fear. These victims of genocide had been psychologically prepared to expect death just for being Tutsi. They were being killed for so long that they were already dead."

I reminded Nkongoli that, for all his hatred of fear, he had himself accepted death before his neighbour urged him to run away. "Yes," he said. "I got tired in the genocide. You struggle so long, then you get tired."

Every Rwandan I spoke with seemed to have a favourite, unanswerable question. For Nkongoli, it was how so many Tutsis had allowed themselves to be killed. For François Xavier Nkurunziza, a Kigali lawyer, whose father was Hutu and whose mother and wife were Tutsi, the question was how so many

---

1   *Providence* God's will, divine intervention.

Hutus had allowed themselves to kill. Nkurunziza had escaped death only by chance as he moved around the country from one hiding place to another, and he had lost many family members. "Conformity is very deep, very developed here," he told me. "In Rwandan history, everyone obeys authority. People revere power, and there isn't enough education. You take a poor, ignorant population, and give them arms, and say, 'It's yours. Kill.' They'll obey. The peasants, who were paid or forced to kill, were looking up to people of higher socio-economic standing to see how to behave. So the people of influence, or the big financiers, are often the big men in the genocide. They may think they didn't kill because they didn't take life with their own hands, but the people were looking to them for their orders. And, in Rwanda, an order can be given very quietly."

As I travelled around the country, collecting accounts of the killing, it almost seemed as if, with the machete, the *masu*—a club studded with nails—a few well-placed grenades, and a few bursts of automatic-rifle fire, the quiet orders of Hutu Power had made the neutron bomb[1] obsolete.

"Everyone was called to hunt the enemy," said Theodore Nyilinkwaya, a survivor of the massacres in his home village of Kimbogo, in the southwestern province of Cyangugu. "But let's say someone is reluctant. Say that guy comes with a stick. They tell him, 'No, get a *masu*.' So, OK, he does, and he runs along with the rest, but he doesn't kill. They say, 'Hey, he might denounce us later. He must kill. Everyone must help to kill at least one person.' So this person who is not a killer is made to do it. And the next day it's become a game for him. You don't need to keep pushing him."

At Nyarubuye, even the little terracotta votive statues[2] in the sacristy had been methodically decapitated. "They were associated with Tutsis," Sergeant Francis explained.

—1999

---

1   *neutron bomb* Thermonuclear weapon that releases a small amount of explosive energy, but an enormous amount of radiation. A neutron bomb does very little damage to infrastructure, but incredible damage to a human population.

2   *votive statues* Statues intended to be used as religious offerings.

David Foster Wallace
1962–2008

David Foster Wallace was an American writer of novels, essays, and short stories. The publication of his novel *Infinite Jest* (1996) catapulted him to national prominence as a writer; in 2005, *Time* magazine included it in their list of the "100 Best English-language Novels Published Since 1923." Wallace's essays—notably "Consider the Lobster" (2004) and "A Supposedly Fun Thing I'll Never Do Again" (1996)—are also widely referenced and anthologized; he has come to be recognized as an important writer in multiple literary genres.

Wallace's father was a professor of philosophy, and his mother was a professor of English; given that background, it is perhaps not surprising that Wallace's approach is both cerebral and consciously literary. His writing style is inquisitive, elliptical, and sometimes playful, but there is a deep seriousness to it; questions about the nature of human experience and the functioning of society lie at the heart of much of his writing, which displays a philosopher's resistance to final and certain answers. He has said that "part of our emergency is that it's so tempting ... to retreat to narrow arrogance, pre-formed positions, rigid filters, the 'moral clarity' of the immature. The alternative is dealing with massive, high-entropy amounts of info and ambiguity and conflict and flux." Reflecting this dilemma, his texts are often wildly discursive—peppered with asides, qualifications, and tangential discussions. *Infinite Jest*, for example, has hundreds of endnotes, many of which are themselves further annotated.

Wallace committed suicide in 2008 after a life-long battle with depression, leaving behind an unfinished manuscript for the novel *The Pale King* (2011). That the unfinished novel became a finalist for the 2012 Pulitzer Prize in fiction testifies to Wallace's important place in the literary world.

How Tracy Austin[1] Broke My Heart

Because I am a long-time rabid fan of tennis in general and Tracy Austin in particular, I've rarely looked forward to reading a sports memoir the way I looked forward to Ms. Austin's *Beyond Center Court: My Story*, ghosted by Christine Brennan and published by Morrow. This is a type of mass-market book—the sports-star-"with"-somebody autobiography—that I seem to have bought and read an awful lot of, with all sorts of ups and downs and ambivalence and embarrassment, usually putting these books under something more

---

1 *Tracy Austin* Retired American tennis player (b. 1962), most active in the late 1970s and early 1980s.

highbrow when I get to the register. I think Austin's memoir has maybe finally broken my jones for the genre, though.

Here's *Beyond Center Court*'s Austin on the first set of her final against Chris Evert[1] at the 1979 US Open: "At 2–3, I broke Chris, then she broke me, and I broke her again, so we were at 4–4."

And on her epiphany after winning that final: "I immediately knew what I had done, which was to win the US Open, and I was thrilled."

Tracy Austin on the psychic rigours of pro competition: "Every professional athlete has to be so fine-tuned mentally."

Tracy Austin on her parents: "My mother and father never, ever pushed me."

Tracy Austin on Martina Navratilova:[2] "She is a wonderful person, very sensitive and caring."

On Billie Jean King:[3] "She also is incredibly charming and accommodating."

On Brooke Shields:[4] "She was so sweet and bright and easy to talk to right away."

Tracy Austin meditating on excellence: "There is that little bit extra that some of us are willing to give and some of us aren't. Why is that? I think it's the challenge to be the best."

You get the idea. On the upside, though, this breathtakingly insipid autobiography can maybe help us understand both the seduction and the disappointment that seem to be built into the mass-market sports memoir. Almost uniformly poor as books, these athletic "My Story"'s sell incredibly well; that's why there are so many of them. And they sell so well because athletes' stories seem to promise something more than the regular old name-dropping celebrity autobiography.

Here is a theory. Top athletes are compelling because they embody the comparison-based achievement we Americans revere—fast*est*, strong*est*—and because they do so in a totally unambiguous way. Questions of the best plumber or best managerial accountant are impossible even to define, whereas the best relief pitcher, free-throw shooter, or female tennis player is, at any given time, a matter of public statistical record. Top athletes fascinate us by appealing to our twin compulsions with competitive superiority and hard data.

---

1   *Chris Evert* Retired American tennis player (b. 1954), active in the 1970s and 1980s.
2   *Martina Navratilova* Retired Czechoslovakian tennis player (b. 1956) who played for the US from 1975 to 2006.
3   *Billie Jean King* Retired American tennis player (b. 1943) who competed from 1959 to 1983.
4   *Brooke Shields* American actor (b. 1965).

Plus they're beautiful: Jordan hanging in midair like a Chagall bride, Sampras laying down a touch volley at an angle that defies Euclid.[1] And they're inspiring. There is about world-class athletes carving out exemptions from physical laws a transcendent beauty that makes manifest God in man. So actually more than one theory, then. Great athletes are profundity in motion. They enable abstractions like *power* and *grace* and *control* to become not only incarnate but televisable. To be a top athlete, performing, is to be that exquisite hybrid of animal and angel that we average unbeautiful watchers have such a hard time seeing in ourselves.

So we want to know them, these gifted, driven physical achievers. We too, as audience, are driven: watching the performance is not enough. We want to get intimate with all that profundity. We want inside them; we want the Story. We want to hear about humble roots, privation, precocity, grim resolve, discouragement, persistence, team spirit, sacrifice, killer instinct, liniment and pain. We want to know how they did it. How many hours a night did the child Bird[2] spend in his driveway hitting jumpers under home-strung floodlights? What ungodly time did Bjorn[3] get up for practice every morning? What exact makes of cars did the Butkus boys work out by pushing up and down Chicago streets?[4] What did Palmer and Brett and Payton[5] and Evert have to give up? And of course, too, we want to know how it *feels*, inside, to be both beautiful and best ("How did it feel to win the big one?"). What combination of blankness and concentration is required to sink a putt or a free-throw for thousands of dollars in front of millions of unblinking eyes? What goes through their minds? Are these athletes real people? Are they even remotely like us? Is their Agony of Defeat anything like our little agonies of daily frustration? And of course what about the Thrill of Victory—what might it feel like to hold up that #1 finger and be able to actually *mean* it?

I am about the same age and played competitive tennis in the same junior ranks as Tracy Austin, half a country away and several plateaus below her.

---

1   *Jordan* Retired American basketball player Michael Jordan (b. 1963); *Chagall* Marc Chagall (1887–1985), a Russian-born Jewish modernist artist whose paintings often include floating figures; *Sampras* Pete Sampras (b. 1971), a retired American tennis player; *Euclid* Greek mathematician (c. 300 BCE) known for his discoveries in the field of geometry.

2   *Bird* Retired American basketball player Larry Bird (b. 1956).

3   *Bjorn* Björn Borg (b. 1956), retired Swedish tennis player.

4   *What exact makes ... Chicago streets?* Reference to American football player Dick Butkus (b. 1942) who during his high school years trained by pushing a car. His brother Ron played college football.

5   *Palmer* Arnold Palmer, famous American golfer (1929–2016); *Brett* George Brett, retired American baseball player (b. 1953); *Payton* Walter Payton, American football player (1954–99).

When we all heard, in 1977, that a California girl who'd just turned fourteen had won a professional tournament in Portland, we weren't so much jealous as agog. None of us could come close to testing even a top eighteen-year-old, much less pro-caliber adults. We started to hunt her up in tennis magazines, search out her matches on obscure cable channels. She was about four foot six and eighty-five pounds. She hit the hell out of the ball and never missed and never choked and had braces and pigtails that swung wildly around as she handed pros their asses. She was the first real child star in women's tennis, and in the late Seventies she was prodigious, beautiful, and inspiring. There was an incongruously adult genius about her game, all the more radiant for her little-girl giggle and silly hair. I remember meditating, with all the intensity a fifteen-year-old can summon, on the differences that kept this girl and me on our respective sides of the TV screen. She was a genius and I was not. How must it have felt? I had some serious questions to ask her. I wanted, very much, her side of it.

So the point, then, about these sports memoirs' market appeal: Because top athletes are profound, because they make a certain type of genius as carnally discernible as it ever can get, these ghostwritten invitations inside their lives and their skulls are terribly seductive for book buyers. Explicitly or not, the memoirs make a promise—to let us penetrate the indefinable mystery of what makes some persons geniuses, semidivine, to share with us the secret and so both to reveal the difference between us and them and to erase it, a little, that difference ... to give us the (we want, expect, only one, the master narrative, the key) Story.

However seductively they promise, though, these autobiographies rarely deliver. And *Beyond Center Court: My Story* is especially bad. The book fails not so much because it's poorly written (which it is—I don't know what ghostwriter Brennan's enhancing function was supposed to be here, but it's hard to see how Austin herself could have done any worse than two hundred dead pages of "Tennis took me like a magic carpet to all kinds of places and all kinds of people" enlivened only by wincers like "Injuries—the signature of the rest of my career—were about to take hold of me"), but because it commits what any college sophomore knows is the capital crime of expository prose: it forgets who it's supposed to be for.

Obviously, a good commercial memoir's first loyalty has got to be to the reader, the person who's spending money and time to access the consciousness of someone he wishes to know and will never meet. But none of *Beyond Center Court's* loyalties are to the reader. The author's primary allegiance seems to be to her family and friends. Whole pages are given over to numbing Academy Award-style tributes to parents, siblings, coaches, trainers, and agents, plus little burbles of praise for pretty much every athlete and celebrity she's ever met. In particular, Austin's account of her own (extremely, transcendently interesting) competitive career keeps digressing into warm fuzzies on each opponent she faces. Typical example: Her third round at 1980's Wimbledon was against American Barbara Potter,[1] who, we learn,

> is a really good person. Barbara was very nice to me through my injuries, sending me books, keeping in touch, and checking to see how I was doing. Barbara definitely was one of the smartest people on the tour; I've heard she's going to college now, which takes a lot of initiative for a woman our age. Knowing Barbara, I'm sure she's working harder than all her fellow students.

But there is also here an odd loyalty to and penchant for the very clichés with which we sports fans weave the veil of myth and mystery that these sports memoirs promise to part for us. It's almost as if Tracy Austin has structured her own sense of her life and career to accord with the formulas of the generic sports bio. We've got the sensitive and doting mother, the kindly dad, the mischievous siblings who treat famous Tracy like just another kid. We've got the ingénue heroine whose innocence is eroded by experience and transcended through sheer grit; we've got the gruff but tender-hearted coach and the coolly skeptical veterans who finally accept the heroine. We've got the wicked, back-stabbing rival (in Pam Shriver,[2] who receives the book's only unfulsome mention). We even get the myth-requisite humble roots. Austin, whose father is a corporate scientist and whose mother is one of those lean tan ladies who seem to spend all day every day at the country club tennis courts, tries to portray her childhood in posh Rolling Hills Estates CA as impoverished: "We had to be frugal in all kinds of ways ... we cut expenses by drinking powdered milk ... we didn't have bacon except on Christmas." Stuff like this seems way out of touch with reality until we realize that the kind of reality the author's chosen to be in touch with here is not just un- but anti-real.

In fact, as unrevealing of character as its press-release tone and generic-myth structure make this memoir, it's the narrator's cluelessness that permits us our only glimpses of anything like a real and faceted life. That is, relief from the book's skewed loyalties can be found only in those places where the author seems unwittingly to betray them. She protests, for instance, repeatedly and with an almost Gertrudian fervour,[3] that her mother "did not force" her into

---

1 *Barbara Potter* Retired American tennis player (b. 1961).

2 *Pam Shriver* Retired American tennis player (b. 1962) who had a well-publicized professional rivalry with Austin.

3 *Gertrudian fervour* Reference to a famous statement made by Queen Gertrude in *Hamlet* 3.2: "The lady doth protest too much, methinks." The "lady" is an actor who, in imitation of the queen herself, makes insincerely overwrought declarations of love for her husband.

tennis at age three, it apparently never occurring to Tracy Austin that a three-year-old hasn't got enough awareness of choices to require any forcing. This was the child of a mom who'd spent the evening before Tracy's birth hitting tennis balls to the family's other four children, three of whom also ended up playing pro tennis. Many of the memoir's recollections of Mrs. Austin seem almost Viennese in their repression[1]—"My mother always made sure I behaved on court, but I never even considered acting up"—and downright creepy are some of the details Austin chooses in order to evince "how nonintense my tennis background really was":

> Everyone thinks every young tennis player is very one-dimensional, which just wasn't true in my case. Until I was fourteen, I never played tennis on Monday.... My mother made sure I never put in seven straight days on the court. She didn't go to the club on Mondays, so we never went there.

It gets weirder. Later in the book's childhood section, Austin discusses her "wonderful friendship" with a man from their country club who "set up ... matches for me against unsuspecting foes in later years and ... won a lot of money from his friends" and, as a token of friendship, "bought me a necklace with a T hanging on it. The T had fourteen diamonds on it." She was apparently ten at this point. As the book's now fully adult Austin analyzes the relationship, "He was a very wealthy criminal lawyer, and I didn't have very much money. With all his gifts for me, he made me feel special." What a guy. Regarding her de facto employment in what is technically known as sports hustling: "It was all in good fun."

In the subsequent section, Austin recalls a 1978 pro tournament in Japan that she hadn't much wanted to enter:

> It was just too far from home and I was tired from the travel grind. They kept offering me more and more money for an appearance fee— well over a hundred thousand dollars—but I said no. Finally, they offered to fly my whole family over. That did it. We went, and I won easily.

Besides displaying an odd financial sense (she won't come for $100,000+, but will come if they add a couple thousand in airfare?), Tracy Austin seems here unaware of the fact that, in the late Seventies, any player who accepted a guaranteed payment just for entering a tournament was in violation of a serious tour rule. The backstory here is that both genders' player associations

---

1   *Viennese in their repression* Reference to Sigmund Freud (1856–1939), a founding figure of psychoanalysis, whose practice was located in Vienna.

had outlawed these payments because they threatened both the real and the perceived integrity of pro tennis. A tournament that has paid some star player a hefty guarantee—wanting her in the draw because her celebrity will help increase ticket sales, corporate sponsorships, TV revenues, etc.—thereafter has an obvious stake in that player's survival in the tournament, and so has an equally obvious interest in keeping her from getting upset by some lesser-known player in the early rounds, which, since matches' linesmen and umpires are employed by the tournament, can lead to shady officiating. And has so led. Far stranger things than a marquee player's receiving a suspicious number of favourable line calls have happened ... though apparently somehow not in Tracy Austin's experience.

The naiveté on display throughout this memoir is doubly confusing. On the one hand, there's little sign in this narrator of anything like the frontal-lobe activity required for outright deception. On the other, Austin's ignorance of her sport's grittier realities seems literally incredible. Random examples. When she sees a player "tank" a 1988 tournament match to make time for a lucrative appearance in a TV ad, Tracy "couldn't believe it.... I had never played with anyone who threw a match before, so it took me a set and a half to realize what was happening." This even though match-tanking had been widely and publicly reported as a dark consequence of skyrocketing exhibition and endorsement fees for at least the eleven years Austin had been in pro tennis. Or, drugs-wise, although problems with everything up to cocaine and heroin in pro tennis had been not only acknowledged but written about in the 1980s,[1] Austin manages to move the reader to both scorn and pity with pronouncements like "I assume players were experimenting with marijuana and certainly were drinking alcohol, but I don't know who or when or where. I wasn't invited to those parties, if they were happening at all. And I'm very glad I wasn't." And so on and so on.

Ultimately, though, what makes *Beyond Center Court* so especially disappointing is that it could have been much more than just another I-was-born-to-play sports memoir. The facts of Tracy Austin's life and its trajectory are almost classically tragic. She was the first of tennis's now-ubiquitous nymphet prodigies, and her rise was meteoric. Picked out of the crowd as a toddler by coaching guru Vic Braden, Austin was on the cover of *World Tennis* magazine at age four. She played her first junior tournament at seven, and by ten she had won the national girls' twelve-and-under championship both indoors and out-and was being invited to play public exhibitions. At thirteen she had won national titles in most junior age-groups, been drafted as a professional by World

---

1   [Wallace's note] AP reporter Michael Mewshaw's *Short Circuit* (Atheneum, 1983) is just one example of national-press stuff about drugs on the tour.

Team Tennis, and appeared on the cover of *Sports Illustrated* under the teaser "A Star Is Born." At fourteen, having chewed up every female in US juniors, she entered the preliminary qualifiers for her first professional tournament and proceeded to win not just the qualifying event but the whole tourney—a feat roughly equivalent to someone who was ineligible for a DMV learner's permit winning the Indianapolis 500. She played Wimbledon at fourteen, turned pro as a ninth-grader, won the US Open at sixteen, and was ranked number one in the world at just seventeen, in 1980. This was the same year her body started to fall apart. She spent the next four years effectively crippled by injuries and bizarre accidents, playing sporadically and watching her ranking plummet, and was for all practical purposes retired from tennis at age twenty-one. In 1989, her one serious attempt at a comeback ended on the way to the US Open, when a speeder ran a red light and nearly killed her. She is now, as of this writing, a professional former sports star, running celebrity clinics for corporate sponsors and doing sad little bits of colour commentary on some of the same cable channels I'd first seen her play on.

What's nearly Greek[1] about her career's arc is that Tracy Austin's most conspicuous virtue, a relentless workaholic perfectionism that combined with raw talent to make her such a prodigious success, turned out to be also her flaw and bane. She was, even after puberty, a tiny person, and her obsessive practice regimen and uncompromising effort in every last match began to afflict her with what sports MDs now know to be simple consequences of hypertrophy and chronic wear: hamstring and hip flexor pulls, sciatica, scoliosis, tendinitis, stress fractures, plantar fasciitis. Then too, since woe classically breeds more woe, she was freak-accident-prone: coaches who fall on her while ice-skating and break her ankle, psychotic chiropractors who pull her spine out of alignment, waiters who splash her with scalding water, colour-blind speeders on the JFK Parkway.

A successful Tracy Austin autobiography, then, could have afforded us plain old plumbers and accountants more than just access to the unquestioned genius of an athletic savant or her high-speed ascent to the top of a univocal, mathematically computed hierarchy. This book could actually have helped us to countenance the sports myth's dark side. The only thing Tracy Austin had ever known how to do, her art—what the tragic-savvy Greeks would have called her *technē*, that state in which Austin's mastery of craft facilitated a communion with the gods themselves—was removed from her at an age when most of us are just starting to think seriously about committing ourselves to some pursuit. This memoir could have been about both the seductive immortality of competitive success and the less seductive but way more significant

---

1   *Greek* I.e., tragic.

fragility and impermanence of all the competitive venues in which mortal humans chase immortality. Austin's story could, since the predicament of a dedicated athletic prodigy washed up at twenty-one differs in nothing more than degree from that of a dedicated CPA[1] and family man dying at sixty-two, have been profound. The book could, since having it all at seventeen and then losing it all by twenty-one because of stuff outside your control is just like death except you have to go on living afterward, have been truly inspirational. And the publisher's flap copy promises just this: "The inspirational story of Tracy Austin's long struggle to find a life beyond championship tennis."

But the publisher's flap copy lies, because it turns out that *inspirational* is being used on the book jacket only in its ad-cliché sense, one basically equivalent to *heartwarming* or *feel-good* or even (God forbid) *triumphant*. Like all good ad clichés, it manages to suggest everything and mean nothing. Honourably used, *to inspire* means, according to Mr. American Heritage,[2] "to animate the mind or emotions of; to communicate by divine influence." Which is to say that *inspirational*, honourably used, describes precisely what a great athlete becomes when she's in the arena performing, sharing the particular divinity she's given her life for, letting people witness concrete, transient instantiations of a grace that for most of us remains abstract and immanent.

Transcendent as were Tracy Austin's achievements on a public court, her autobiography does not come anywhere close to honouring the promise of its flap copy's "inspirational." Because forget divine—there's not even a recognizable human being in here. And this isn't just because of clunky prose or luxated[3] structure. The book is inanimate because it communicates no real feeling and so gives us no sense of a conscious person. There's nobody at the other end of the line. Every emotionally significant moment or event or development gets conveyed in either computeresque staccato or else a prepackaged PR-speak whose whole function is (think about it) to deaden feeling. See, for instance, Austin's account of the moment when she has just beaten a world-class adult to win her first professional tournament:

> It was a tough match and I simply outlasted her. I was beginning to get a reputation for doing that. When you play from the baseline, perseverance is everything. The prize money for first place was twenty-eight thousand dollars.[4]

---

1   *CPA* Certified Public Accountant.
2   *Mr. American Heritage* I.e., *The American Heritage Dictionary*.
3   *luxated* Dislocated.
4   [Wallace's note] Or listen again to her report of how winning her first US Open felt: "I immediately knew what I had done, which was to win the US Open, and I was thrilled." This line haunts me; it's like the whole letdown of the book boiled down into one dead bite.

Or check out the book's description of her career's tragic climax. After working for five years to make a comeback and then, literally on the way to Flushing Meadow's National Tennis Center, getting sideswiped by a van and having her leg shattered through sheer bad luck, Tracy Austin was now permanently finished as a world-class athlete, and had then to lie for weeks in traction and think about the end of the only life she'd ever known. In *Beyond Center Court*, Austin's inspirational prose-response to this consists of quoting Leo Buscaglia,[1] reporting on her newfound enthusiasm for shopping, and then giving us an excruciating chapter-long list of every celebrity she's ever met.

Of course, neither Austin nor her book is unique. It's hard not to notice the way this same air of robotic banality suffuses not only the sports-memoir genre but also the media rituals in which a top athlete is asked to describe the content or meaning of his *technē*. Turn on any post-contest TV interview: "Kenny, how did it feel to make that sensational game-winning shoestring catch in the end zone with absolutely no I mean *zero* time remaining on the clock?" "Well, Frank, I was just real pleased. I was real happy and also pleased. We've all worked hard and come a long way as a team, and it's always a good feeling to be able to contribute." "Mark, you've now homered in your last eight straight at-bats and lead both leagues in RBIs—any comment?" "Well, Bob, I'm just trying to take it one pitch at a time. I've been focusing on the fundamentals, you know, and trying to make a contribution, and all of us know we've got to take it one game at a time and hang in there and not look ahead and just basically do the best we can at all times." This stuff is stupefying, and yet it also seems to be inevitable, maybe even necessary. The baritones in network blazers keep coming up after games, demanding of physical geniuses these recombinant strings[2] of dead clichés, strings that after a while start to sound like a strange kind of lullaby, and which of course no network would solicit and broadcast again and again if there weren't a large and serious audience out here who find the banalities right and good. As if the emptiness in these athletes' descriptions of their feelings confirmed something we need to believe.

All right, so the obvious point: Great athletes usually turn out to be stunningly inarticulate about just those qualities and experiences that constitute their fascination. For me, though, the important question is why this is always so bitterly disappointing. And why I keep buying these sports memoirs with expectations that my own experience with the genre should long ago have modified ... and why I nearly always feel thwarted and pissed when I finish

---

1   *Leo Buscaglia* American motivational speaker, also known as "Dr. Love" (1924–98).
2   *recombinant strings* Reference to recombinant DNA, which can be made by joining together material taken from pre-existing DNA strands.

them. One sort of answer, of course, is that commercial autobiographies like these promise something they cannot deliver: personal and verbal access to an intrinsically public and performative kind of genius. The problem with this answer is that I and the rest of the US book market aren't that stupid—if impossible promises were all there was to it, we'd catch on after a while, and it would stop being so profitable for publishers to churn these memoirs out.

Maybe what keeps us buying in the face of constant disappointment is some deep compulsion both to experience genius in the concrete and to universalize genius in the abstract. Real indisputable genius is so impossible to define, and true *technē* so rarely visible (much less televisable), that maybe we automatically expect people who are geniuses as athletes to be geniuses also as speakers and writers, to be articulate, perceptive, truthful, profound. If it's just that we naively expect geniuses-in-motion to be also geniuses-in-reflection, then their failure to be that shouldn't really seem any crueler or more disillusioning than Kant's glass jaw or Eliot's[1] inability to hit the curve.

For my part, though, I think there's something deeper, and scarier, that keeps my hope one step ahead of past experience as I make my way to the bookstore's register. It remains very hard for me to reconcile the vapidity of Austin's narrative mind, on the one hand, with the extraordinary mental powers that are required by world-class tennis, on the other. Anyone who buys the idea that great athletes are dim should have a close look at an NFL playbook, or at a basketball coach's diagram of a 3–2 zone trap ... or at an archival film of Ms. Tracy Austin repeatedly putting a ball in a court's corner at high speed from seventy-eight feet away, with huge sums of money at stake and enormous crowds of people watching her do it. Ever try to concentrate on doing something difficult with a crowd of people watching? ... worse, with a crowd of spectators maybe all vocally hoping you fail so that their favourite will beat you? In my own comparatively low-level junior matches, before audiences that rarely hit three digits, it used to be all I could do to manage my sphincter. I would drive myself crazy: "... but what if I double-fault here and go down a break with all these folks watching? ... don't think about it ... yeah but except if I'm consciously not thinking about it then doesn't part of me have to think about it in order for me to remember what I'm not supposed to think about? ... shut *up*, quit thinking about it and serve the goddamn ball ... except how can I even be talking to myself about not thinking about it unless I'm still aware of what it is I'm talking about not thinking about?" and so on. I'd get divided, paralyzed. As most ungreat athletes do. Freeze up, choke. Lose our

---

1 *Kant* German philosopher Immanuel Kant (1724–1804), a central figure in modern philosophy; *Eliot* T.S. Eliot (1888–1965), a prominent Anglo-American modernist poet.

focus. Become self-conscious. Cease to be wholly present in our wills and choices and movements.

It is not an accident that great athletes are often called "naturals," because they can, in performance, be totally present: they can proceed on instinct and muscle-memory and autonomic[1] will such that agent and action are one. Great athletes can do this even—and, for the truly great ones like Borg and Bird and Nicklaus[2] and Jordan and Austin, *especially*—under wilting pressure and scrutiny. They can withstand forces of distraction that would break a mind prone to self-conscious fear in two.

The real secret behind top athletes' genius, then, may be as esoteric and obvious and dull and profound as silence itself. The real, many-veiled answer to the question of just what goes through a great player's mind as he stands at the center of hostile crowd-noise and lines up the free-throw that will decide the game might well be: *nothing at all.*

How can great athletes shut off the Iago-like[3] voice of the self? How can they bypass the head and simply and superbly act? How, at the critical moment, can they invoke for themselves a cliché as trite as "One ball at a time" or "Gotta concentrate here," and *mean* it, and then *do* it? Maybe it's because, for top athletes, clichés present themselves not as trite but simply as true, or perhaps not even as declarative expressions with qualities like depth or triteness or falsehood or truth but as simple imperatives that are either useful or not and, if useful, to be invoked and obeyed and that's all there is to it.

What if, when Tracy Austin writes that after her 1989 car crash, "I quickly accepted that there was nothing I could do about it," the statement is not only true but *exhaustively descriptive* of the entire acceptance process she went through? Is someone stupid or shallow because she can say to herself that there's nothing she can do about something bad and so she'd better accept it, and thereupon simply accept it with no more interior struggle? Or is that person maybe somehow natively wise and profound, enlightened in the child-like way some saints and monks are enlightened?

This is, for me, the real mystery—whether such a person is an idiot or a mystic or both and/or neither. The only certainty seems to be that such a person does not produce a very good prose memoir. That plain empirical fact may be the best way to explain how Tracy Austin's actual history can be so com-

---

1   *autonomic* Involuntary; the autonomic nervous system regulates bodily functions such as breathing and digestion.

2   *Nicklaus* Retired American golfer (b. 1940), generally considered to be one of the best golfers of all time.

3   *Iago-like* Reference to the Shakespearean antagonist from *Othello* (c. 1603–04). Iago convinces Othello that his wife is having an affair and in doing so initiates a chain of events that leads to Othello's downfall.

pelling and important and her verbal account of that history not even alive. It may also, in starting to address the differences in communicability between thinking and doing and between doing and being, yield the key to why top athletes' autobiographies are at once so seductive and so disappointing for us readers. As is so often SOP[1] with the truth, there's a cruel paradox involved. It may well be that we spectators, who are not divinely gifted as athletes, are the only ones able truly to see, articulate, and animate the experience of the gift we are denied. And that those who receive and act out the gift of athletic genius must, perforce, be blind and dumb about it—and not because blindness and dumbness are the price of the gift, but because they are its essence.

—1994

---

1   *SOP* Standard Operating Procedure.

Kamal Al-Solaylee
b. 1964

A Canadian author and professor of journalism at Ryerson University, Kamal Al-Solaylee is also a political activist who seeks to lend his voice to the "millions of darker-skinned people who ... have missed out on the economic and political gains of the post-industrial world and are now clamouring for their fair share of the social mobility, equality, and freedom." His journalism, which includes extensive TV, film, and theatre criticism as well as reportage on international political events, has appeared in *The Globe and Mail*, the *Toronto Star*, the *National Post*, and *The Walrus*.

Although born in the city of Aden, which is now a part of Yemen, Al-Solaylee grew up in Beirut and Cairo as the youngest of 11 children. He returned briefly to Yemen at age 22, but soon left for London, England, both to complete his PhD in English and to escape Yemen's homophobic laws. Al-Solaylee's first book, *Intolerable: A Memoir of Extremes* (2012), recounts his experiences as a gay man growing up in the Middle East in the midst of political changes that brought increasing violence and repression. In this text, he urges young people struggling to live within intolerant environments to remain hopeful in spite of the challenges they face on a daily basis. "You can overcome all that—unfortunately, you may have to get away, as you can't expect the whole culture to change around you."

Al-Solaylee's second book, *Brown: What Being Brown in the World Today Means (to Everyone)* (2016), contemplates brownness as a racial identity and addresses the precarious situation of brown people in the contemporary world. *Brown* was shortlisted for the Governor General's Award.

from *Brown: What Being Brown in the World Today Means (to Everyone)*

I remember the moment I realized I was brown. My brown face, my brown legs and my curly black hair began to weigh on my mind in a way they never had before. Let me take you back to Cairo, early 1974. For several days, one of Egypt's two state television channels had been promoting the small-screen premiere of *Oliver!*, the 1968 film version of the British musical. It was a big deal in Cairo, and probably an omen for a city whose future poverty levels and income inequality would make Victorian London look like a socialist paradise. I write that with the full benefit of hindsight. I was a nine-year-old boy growing up as part of an expatriate Yemeni family, so I can't say that I knew much about the economy or the distribution of wealth back then.

I can't remember why I decided to stay up so late on a school night to watch a period musical about English orphans, pickpocketing gangs and prostitutes with teachable-moment altruism. I had but a passing familiarity with the story, and Western musicals were an artistic taste I had yet to acquire. (I caught up with them as part of an education in all things camp and old Hollywood when I came out as a gay man in my early twenties.)

The film aired just a few months short of my tenth birthday. Life in Egypt had returned to normal after three weeks of fighting and humiliating—or so the propaganda machine would have Egyptians believe—the Israeli army in a war that had started on October 6, 1973.[1] The end of hostilities meant a return to regular programming and a break from the rotation of military- and nationalist-themed songs and documentaries. My father, a lifelong anglophile, probably insisted that we children watch this slice of Merrie Olde England—a display of all things English that only a hardcore colonial like him was permitted to find jolly or nostalgic.

About twenty minutes into the film, though, he lost interest. You could always tell when something he longed for turned out to be a dud, because he'd start talking through it. Probably he hadn't realized that this was a musical version of Dickens's *Oliver Twist*. He didn't particularly like musicals, unless they starred Fred Astaire and Ginger Rogers,[2] his childhood idols.

I, on the other hand, trembled on the inside as I watched the film. My world tilted in that moment, and I'm not sure it's been set right since.

Every time the camera zoomed in on the face of the young actor playing Oliver, Mark Lester, I became painfully aware of how different my own face looked. As the youngest child in a large family, I was adored by my older siblings—the sweet baby boy. But the more I gazed at Lester's face, the less I felt any kind of pride in my looks, and my innocence slipped from under me in the process. He was just too beautiful, too angelic-looking. It defied the laws of nature as I knew them then. I don't think I viewed him in any sexual terms, even though my own awareness of my same-sex desire predated that evening by a few years. I saw it as a skin-to-skin and not boy-to-boy attraction. He had what, all of a sudden, I desired.

If my lifelong journey with physical insecurities and differences in skin colours can be traced to a single moment in time, it is that one. Most children in my immediate circle in downtown Cairo looked like variations of me. Sure,

---

1   *a war that ... October 6, 1973* The 1973 Arab-Israeli War, also called the Yom Kippur War, was a 20-day conflict between Israel and an alliance of primarily Egyptian and Syrian forces. Though Israel is generally recognized as having won the war, Egypt and Syria saw significant victories early in the conflict.

2   *Fred Astaire and Ginger Rogers* Famous dance partners who starred in a series of Hollywood musicals in the 1930s and 1940s.

some bragged about their very light complexion or their ash-blond hair, but no one came close to Mark Lester in brightness, whiteness, holiness. Looking at him, I felt like a lost soul, forever damned by a dark skin.

To be beautiful—to be adorably mischievous—a person needed to look like Lester. His light, shiny hair and his perfectly proportioned features forced me to rush to the bathroom to look at my own face and tousle my own hair. Probably for the first time in my life, all I saw reflected in that mirror was a black, dandruff-prone and curly mane; a big, flat nose; and ears that looked more clown-like than child-like. The hair could be trimmed or straightened, I consoled myself, and perhaps my nose and ears weren't all that unshapely. But there was one thing I couldn't rationalize away: my brown skin. What was I to do with this dark mass? How could I ever catch up with Lester's whiteness, which was the essence of his impossible beauty? If I scrubbed my face with soap ten, twenty times a day, would it get lighter and whiter? What about the rest of my body? How many showers a day would that be? How do you wash the brown away?

I needed answers. I needed help. I got neither.

I felt cursed with this brownness that I'd inherited from my passes-for-white father and my dark brown mother, who came from a Bedouin sheep-tending family in the southern tip of Yemen. My ten siblings displayed a variety of skin shades—some closer to my father's, some to my mother's. I came in between. Standard brown. Egyptians had coined a word for people like me: *asmarany*. It meant someone with a dark complexion, possibly from sustained exposure to the sun, and probably from working cotton fields or construction sites. There was pride in being sun-kissed—it was a symbol of hard work and stamina. In the nationalist period immediately after the 1952 revolution, which eventually severed the country's ties to the British and Ottoman empires, popular musicians wrote songs about the beauty of *asmarany* people. I recently came across one from the late Lebanese singer Sabah, in which she defended her love for an Egyptian *asmarany* man by insisting that his dark skin was actually the secret to his beauty. The song title translates to "So What If He's Brown-Skinned?"

But I didn't comprehend brown skin in that positive sense that night in 1974, or in the many years that followed. Popular music aside, Egypt was teeming with images that not so subtly equated lighter skin with social refinement and physical perfection—possibly, and with hindsight again, my first encounter with white privilege. It's still difficult to fathom how a country at the heart of the Middle East—one that led the way in pan-Arabism and post-colonialism—would be the custodian of a tradition in which the predominant skin colour was relegated to an inferior social position. To be white or very fair-skinned was to win the genetic lottery, and the few who claimed their tickets ensured that social traditions perpetuated this "understanding." Egyptian cinema, the Hollywood of the Arab world, featured a number of leading men and women whose lighter skin was the most desirable part of their physical package.

Egyptian TV commercials and print advertisements of the time sold a bourgeois, consumer-friendly lifestyle through lighter skin, which they promoted as aspirational for the millions of rich *and* poor locals. I don't recall seeing brown-skinned women or men—certainly no dark brown or Nubian-black models—in any of the advertising I grew up watching in the Middle East. Only *National Geographic*-style travel posters in hotels or airports sold an "authentic" Egyptian experience to Western tourists. With the exception of their white teeth, those smiling faces were enveloped in darkness, as if to fulfill tourist fantasies of an exotic journey into the tip of Africa. From my travels over the past few years, I can safely say that selling whiteness and selling out brownness is a long and still-thriving tradition in the Middle East, the Gulf and Southeast Asia. In Dubai, white, European-looking faces promote everything from multimillion-dollar condos to fast-fashion outlets like Zara and H&M. In the odd instance when advertisers deign to use Arab models, it looks like a generous dollop of white paint has been applied to their faces. Not even white people are *that* white.

Many of these images, I suppose, had entered my subconscious before that night watching *Oliver!* Yet somehow those close-ups of Lester's face served as the catalyst, triggering a lifelong awareness of my skin colour as my gateway to seeing the world and being seen by it. This played out in a variety of social and political contexts over decades and across many countries. Wherever I lived or travelled to, my skin awareness followed, a shadow of my shadow. I don't think I'll ever be able to separate myself from it, but I can unpack its meanings, or at least some of them, with a look back at my own and other people's journeys with brownness.

Around 1979, when I was in high school and trying (and failing dismally) to experiment with heterosexuality, a beautiful young Egyptian girl made it clear that we couldn't date—and I use that very North American term loosely and anachronistically—because her mother would find me too dark. My skin tones would pollute the gene pool of a bourgeois Egyptian family that took pride in its lighter skin, its biggest asset in the marriage and social markets.

As a teenager, I lived in fear of being given any item of clothing in red. My parents had taught me and my siblings to show gratitude by using gifts from family and friends as soon as possible. But a popular Egyptian saying at the time went something like this: "Get an *asmarany* to wear red and you'll make people laugh at him." In plainer words, he'll look like a monkey's behind.

The association strikes me as profoundly racist now, but what really sank in for me at the time was the idea that some colours were off limits for me—not because they didn't complement my skin tones but because they made me look like a beast.

My awareness of being brown would become entrenched a few years later, when I moved to the West. As a foreign student in the United Kingdom in the early 1990s, I was called "Paki" more than once. I often wanted to shout back that I wasn't actually Pakistani. It had never occurred to me that I would be lumped with South Asians on the racial-slur spectrum, because I had thought of myself as lighter-skinned than most of them. They were dark brown; I was light brown. Couldn't these racists tell the difference?

As a Canadian citizen in the aftermath of September 11, I learned to accept racial profiling as part of my everyday reality as a brown male—at least until I reached my late forties and started looking too haggard to be a troublemaker or a jihadist. Terrorism is a young man's business.

When I was a (younger) gay man visiting largely white bars and clubs in North America and Europe, I felt either desired or rejected because of my skin tone. (It depended on the evening and the crowd.) Even during a brief 2008 visit to Buenos Aires, the heart of what I thought was brown Latino country, I apparently went to the wrong bar, the one frequented by Argentines of European descent. I'd never felt more like a pariah in my entire life, and that included the time I went on a London-bound bus trip to visit the British Parliament with a group of Young Conservatives in 1991. Getting ignored in bars didn't rankle me that much in general, but this felt more like invisibility—a complete erasure of every part of me, not just my skin. An Argentine friend told me the next day that I should have gone to a more working-class bar where brown and black gay men, local and international, socialized. Being of a lower class made it acceptable to be of darker skin, too.

As a gay man who came of age in the 1980s, between the AIDS epidemic and the perfect-body cult with its white assumptions, I had already found it hard to avoid pondering how skin colour set people apart from (or invited them into) the inner circles of fabulousness. Whenever the models for crotch-enhancing underwear or phone sex in bar rags weren't white, they were black. *Very* black. Desire came in two colours only, and mine wasn't one of them. And although many white gay men of my generation fetishized darker-skinned males, projecting images of hyper-masculinity on, say, Latinos and Middle Easterners, the latter rarely crossed over from the "ethnic porn" aisle to the mainstream of gay sexuality.

Not all my personal experiences of being brown have carried negative undertones, however. In the winter, my white friends tell me they envy my complexion because it doesn't turn as pasty and washed-out as theirs does. (I never notice the difference and have always thought they were being too self-conscious about their own skin, the poor dears.) In parts of New York, I often take advantage of being perceived as *not black*. I've had no problem hailing cabs late at night in Manhattan or asking for directions from passersby. In the hierarchy of skin shades, being brown occupies the comfortable middle space, the buffer—we are not as privileged as whites but not as criminalized as blacks.

My own shade of brown is not fixed—it gets darker in the summer and lighter in the winter. Like many middle-class people who trace their origins to the Global South, I tend to avoid the sun wherever I go. (I used to wonder why white people went to such great lengths to get a tan. All those hours on the beach, and for what?) I'm over fifty now and have never once sunbathed in a park on a summer day, taken a beach holiday or set foot inside a tanning salon. It's a brown-people thing. And a class one, too. The darker you turn, the more you look like the working masses—or so I've been trained to think since childhood. More than forty years later, I can still hear my sister Hoda admonishing me for playing under Cairo's blazing sun: "You'll look like a *khadaam* [a servant]." Summer or winter, it didn't matter—the sun became a year-round enemy to the lightness of our skin. Whenever my brother Wahby, the darkest of the eleven children, misbehaved or showed his stubborn streak, my mother would chide him with the word *abd*, Arabic for "slave."

If you're brown, it's hard to deprogram yourself from thinking such seemingly superficial but nonetheless existential questions as: Am I too dark? If I get darker, will I lose my social position? If I avoid the sun forever, will I pass for white, or at least southern European? Brown people can turn their in-between skin into a back door to Europeanness and whiteness. They just need to stick to the very southern parts of the continent.

Over the years, I've heard similar stories from several Hispanic, Arab, South and East Asian, and North African friends. We live in our skin, our largest human organ—and possibly the biggest prison of them all.

I recall a Syrian student who refused to join a picnic with other doctoral candidates from the graduate club at Nottingham University (where I was doing my PhD in Victorian literature) because the sun was too bright that particular July weekend. It was the very reason the British students had planned the outing. Another friend of Indian descent invited me to a curry restaurant in her hometown of Leicester, where she proceeded to treat the dark-skinned waiter—Bangladeshi, if I remember correctly—abominably, dismissing my concerns on the grounds that "darkies" like him were used to this abusive behaviour from the community. It was the first time I'd heard the word "darkie." It never left my consciousness. It had a negativity that my then favourite word, "swarthy," didn't. Swarthy implied exoticism, even desire.

In 2004, when I told an Indian friend in Toronto that I'd booked my first-ever trip to Southeast Asia, she asked if I could bring her back some skin-whitening creams. (The Toronto summer sun turned her brown skin a shade too dark for her comfort.) Had I known such concoctions existed, I would have forked over all my allowances and begged for more to get hold of them in the post-*Oliver!* years. I spent three weeks travelling through the gorgeous landscapes of Singapore, Malaysia and Thailand on that trip, but I tracked the journey less by the change in scenery and local cultures and more by the gradual darkening of my skin. I didn't want to be a darkie.

Facing a mirror and examining not just my hair but my exact shade of brown turned into a lifelong preoccupation. You may think that I'm operating at the shallow end of life. But I know I'm not alone. Who hasn't obsessed about their body, hair, face, skin—whatever colour the latter may be? Didn't James Joyce write that "modern man has an epidermis rather than a soul"?[1]

It took time to see beyond the exterior. But over many years, I've identified with and felt strengthened by narratives that transcended appearance, including the civil rights, feminist, gay liberation and social justice movements. I experienced a political awakening from the outside in. And while this book is not a chronicle of that journey, it wouldn't have been written without the realization that my struggles to feel at ease in the skin I'm in reflect global issues and trends that go beyond the personal. Everywhere I looked, every story I heard, all but confirmed the prejudices and advantages that a skin tone can inflict or bestow on individuals, communities and nations. The concept of race as biologically determined may have been banished from all but the most extreme corners of politics, but the experiences of racialization, of being judged—literally, in the case of the US legal system—on the colour of one's skin, continue. And the closer I looked, the more I noticed the unique place that brown skin occupied in the global story of race relations and perceptions.

I believe there's a certain collective experience that unites people of brown skin—brown people—despite their geographic, ethnic, national and cultural differences. We are united (and divided) by the fact that we're not white. Or black. Millions of us may be living in East Asia, but we're not ethnic Chinese either. We are billions of people spread across the world and better known as Middle Easterners, Latin Americans, North Africans, and South and Southeast Asians.

To be brown in the world today is to recognize narratives and life experiences that unfold with striking similarities despite different settings and

---

1   *modern man ... a soul* See Joyce's essay "The Universal Literary Influence of the Renaissance" (1912).

contexts. These are not exclusive to brown people, but they take place with such frequency and in such concentration among us that we can claim some ownership of them. Uppermost among them—and a particular focus of this book [*Brown*]—are the experiences of the brown migrant and immigrant. Although each term refers to a specific group of people—migrants move out of desperation, while immigrants relocate in pursuit of better lives—the lines between the two continue to be blurred as war and ecological disasters ravage parts of the Global South.

We're on the move, uprooted, always elsewhere, a sizable portion of 244 million people living outside our countries of birth (a figure, the UN projects, that will reach 590 million by 2050). You'll find us at airports, border crossings and ports, aboard trains, ferries and cars, with our luggage and boxes held together by duct tape and sheer willpower. Our dreams and trepidations dominate this endless journey. Some of us may have our papers in order as we cross borders, but many of us hope to enter other countries, other worlds, using false claims (visiting family) or on humanitarian grounds (seeking refugee status at point of entry). Some of us are surgeons, university professors, investors, tech wizards and creative artists, but many, many more have found a calling in life by doing the work that affluent local people no longer wish to do. We're here to build high-rises, work in kitchens, clean homes, tend to the young and elderly, pick fruits and vegetables from fields (and stock them in supermarkets), and drive everyone home after a night of boozing.

The brown immigrants trigger conversations and political strategies from which their black, East Asian and white counterparts are spared—at least at this moment in time. Those of us who are Muslim live under constant suspicion for the religion we follow. As the 2015 federal elections in Canada proved, when a political party lags behind in the polls, nothing whips its base into a frenzy of racial discrimination faster than depicting Muslims as a stain on Canadian values.[1]

The association of brown people with transient labour is not limited to the white, developed world. As I will show in this book, the lives of some brown migrant workers reach certain intensity in places as far apart as the Caribbean and the Far East, and even *within* other brown nations. It's hard not to think of the brown South Asian worker without considering the thousands of construction workers from Nepal, Sri Lanka and Bangladesh whose blood and sweat have gone into virtually every building, high- or low-rise, in Dubai and Qatar. It's in Dubai, too, that middle-class immigrants from the Middle East

---

1   *2015 federal elections … values* The then-ruling Conservative party promised to establish a police hotline to allow citizens to report "barbaric cultural practices." This proposal was widely condemned as Islamophobic.

and the South Asian subcontinent have for decades kept the schools, banks, hospitals, hotels, food courts and malls running—without ever being afforded the benefits of citizenship.

We are lured to do the work in good times—until the economic bubble bursts. Then we turn into the job stealers, the welfare scammers and the undocumented. Two days before Christmas 2014, the Malaysian government mobilized its military aircraft to deport hundreds of undocumented Indonesian workers. Other illegal workers in Malaysia come from India, Bangladesh and Nepal, and at least one report estimates their numbers at six million. The boom in the Malaysian economy in the decades prior to the financial crisis of 2008 led to a vast improvement in lifestyle for locals. Millions joined the middle classes (by Malaysian standards), and then farmed out work on plantations and in restaurants and homes to other, less privileged brown people from the region. Many collected garbage or cleaned bathrooms in the upscale malls that earned Kuala Lumpur a spot on CNN's list of the top-five shopping destinations in Asia. In early 2015, Indonesian diplomats formally protested to the Malaysian government after a print ad for a vacuum cleaner featured the tagline "Fire Your Indonesian Maid Now."

Men made up the majority of the deported, but brown women are on the move, too. The brown migrant worker, whether in the West or the Gulf States or East Asia, is best symbolized by the millions of Filipina nannies, caregivers and domestic workers. Their tales of family separation, harsh living conditions, exploitation and physical abuse transcend borders. According to one labour organization, employers and recruiters who underpay or fail to pay domestics walk away with about $8 billion a year in illegal profits. As one domestic in Hong Kong told me, the jackpot was a permit to work for a white family in the United States or Canada. (In the informal poll of worst-possible destinations that I conducted with a group of domestic workers, also in Hong Kong, Saudi Arabia topped the list.)

But even in open, tolerant Canada, assumptions about skin colour and specific lines of work are made. I learned that while taking my dog for a walk a few days after moving into my condo building in midtown Toronto. A resident stopped me to ask if I had a business card. I couldn't understand why until it dawned on me that she thought I was a dog walker. Her mind couldn't conceive of the possibility that I was also a resident. She read my skin tone as my identity: worker, and low-paid at that. Many of my aging neighbours rely on a revolving cast of caregivers, helpers and cleaners—most of whom are brown. They hail from the Philippines, Central or South America, and occasionally Somalia or Ethiopia. I see and say hello to so many of them every morning, but I've never once learned their names and have often mixed up which caregiver works for which neighbour on my own floor.

I suspect I'm not alone. How many of us know the name of the Colombian or Nepalese cleaning lady we see only when we work late in the office? Brown people are everywhere and yet somehow remain invisible or nameless. But life and the global economy would come to a halt if the mass relocation of these workers—cleaners, domestic workers, security guards, maintenance staff, cooks, pedicurists, construction workers, farmhands and cashiers who ask for your loyalty card when you pay for toothpaste and toilet paper—were to stop. We keep the world running as we ourselves are run out from one spot to another. The words "work permit," "legal status" and "permanent visa" are music to our brown ears. The notes get discordant when we hear "minimum wage or below," "dormitory-style accommodation," "withholding passports" or "deportation." Our lives unfold as a constant battle to move from the second set of words to the first, to lend legitimacy and a home base to our journeys.

We know (or at least hope) that legitimacy brings with it political recognition and social acceptance. Others in the Western world have reached a similar conclusion.

—2016

Miriam Toews
b. 1964

"This town is so severe. And silent. It makes me crazy, the silence." So the teenaged Nomi Nickel describes her home town, the Mennonite community of East Village, in Miriam Toews's fourth novel, *A Complicated Kindness* (2004). That book, which was a best-seller and winner of the Governor General's Award, established Toews as a major figure on the Canadian literary landscape. Like most of her other work, it draws powerfully upon Toews's experience growing up in the town of Steinbach, Manitoba. In Toews's fiction the currents of comedy are often as powerful as those of sadness or despair—and both often spring from her religious upbringing. "We're Mennonites," Nomi tells the reader: "As far as I know, we are the most embarrassing sub-sect of people to belong to if you're a teenager."

Toews is known for her sure touch with wry comedy, but her life and her work have also been touched by tragedy. In 1998, Toews's father committed suicide after a lifelong battle with bipolar disorder. Toews paid tribute to him in an essay on the connections between his Mennonite beliefs and his struggles with depression; "A Father's Faith" (1999) was first published in a magazine, and later reprinted in an anthology of women's writing, *Dropped Threads* (2001). Her full-length memoir, *Swing Low: A Life* (2000), was told from the point of view of her father. Her 2008 novel, *The Flying Troutmans*, also centres on mental illness. It tells the story of narrator Hattie's road trip with her niece and nephew, whose mother (Hattie's sister) suffers from severe depression.

In 2007 Toews was asked to star in Mexican director Carlo Reygadas' *Silent Light* (2007), a film set in a Mennonite community in Northern Mexico. Toews drew on that experience for her 2011 novel, *Irma Voth*, which concerns two young women whose family has moved from the Canadian prairie to a Mennonite community in Mexico; the arrival of a film crew who plan to make a film about the community becomes the catalyst for change.

In describing what she writes about, Toews has sometimes emphasized simple contrasts. In a 2008 interview with *Quill & Quire*, for example, she summed things up in this way: "Life is funny and life is sad. Life is comic and life is tragic. It's a breeze and it's hell." In "A Father's Faith," though—as in the best of her fiction—the interest comes less from simple oppositions than from Toews's sure feel for complications and for subtleties.

A Father's Faith

On the morning of May 13, 1998, my father woke up, had breakfast, got dressed and walked away from the Steinbach Bethesda Hospital, where he had been a patient for two and a half weeks. He walked through his beloved hometown, along Hespeler Road, past the old farmhouse where his mother had lived with her second husband, past the water tower, greeting folks in his loud, friendly voice, wishing them well. He passed the site on First Street where the house in which my sister and I grew up once stood. He walked down Main Street, past the Mennonite church where, throughout his life, he had received countless certificates for perfect attendance, past Elmdale School where he had taught grade six for forty years.

As he walked by his home on Brandt Road, he saw his old neighbour Bill sitting in his lawn chair. He waved and smiled again, then he continued on past the cemetery where his parents were buried, and the high school his daughters had attended, and down Highway 52, out of town, past the Frantz Motor Inn, which is just outside the town limits because it serves alcohol and Steinbach is a dry town. He kept walking until he got too tired, so he hitched a ride with a couple of guys who were on their way to buy a fishing licence in the small village of Woodridge on the edge of the Sandilands Forest.

The sun would have been very warm by the time they dropped him off, and he would have taken off his stylish cap and wiped his brow with the back of his hand. I'm sure he thanked them profusely, perhaps offering them ten dollars for their trouble, and then he walked the short distance to the café near the railroad tracks, the place he and my mom would sometimes go for a quiet coffee and a change of scenery. He would have been able to smell the clover growing in the ditches beside the tracks and between the ties. He may have looked down the line and remembered that the train would be coming from Ontario, through Warroad, Minnesota, on its way to Winnipeg.

A beautiful young woman named Stephanie was just beginning her shift and she spoke to him through the screen door at the side of the restaurant. Yes, she said, the train will be here soon. And my dad smiled and thanked her, and mentioned that he could hear the whistle. Moments later, he was dead.

Steinbach is an easy forty-minute drive from Winnipeg, east on the Trans-Canada, then south on Highway 12. On the way into town there's a sign proclaiming "Jesus Saves." On the way back to the city just off Highway 12 there's another that says, "Satan is Real. You Can't Be Neutral. Choose Now." The town has recently become a city of 8,500 people, two-thirds of whom are Mennonite, so it's not surprising that about half of the twenty-four churches are Mennonite and conservative. There is a Catholic church too, but it's new and I'm not sure exactly where it is. A little way down from the bowling alley

I can still make out my name on the sidewalk, carved in big bold letters when I was ten and marking my territory.

My town made sense to me then. For me it was a giant playground where my friends and I roamed freely, using the entire town in a game of arrows—something like hide-and-seek—for which my dad, the teacher, provided boxes and boxes of fresh new chalk and invaluable tips. He had, after all, played the same game in the same town many years before.

At six p.m. the siren would go off at the firehall, reminding all the kids to go home for supper, and at nine p.m. it was set off again, reminding us to go home to bed. I had no worries, and no desire ever to leave this place where everyone knew me. If they couldn't remember my name, they knew I was the younger daughter of Mel and Elvira Toews, granddaughter of C.T. Loewen and Henry Toews, from the Kleine Gemeinde congregation, and so on and so on. All the kids in town, other than the church-sponsored Laotians who came over in the seventies, could be traced all the way back to the precise Russian veldt their great-grandparents had emigrated from. They were some of the thousands of Mennonites who came to Manitoba in the late 1800s to escape religious persecution. They were given free land and a promise that they could, essentially, do their own thing without interference. They wanted to keep the world away from their children and their children away from the world. Naturally it was an impossible ideal.

As I grew older, I became suspicious and critical and restless and angry. Every night I plotted my escape. I imagined that Barkman's giant feed mill on Main Street, partially visible from my bedroom window, was a tall ship that would take me away some day. I looked up places like Hollywood and Manhattan and Venice and Montreal in my Childcraft encyclopedias. I begged my sister to play, over and over, the sad songs from her Jacques Brel piano book, and I'd light candles and sing along, wearing a Pioneer Girls tam[1] on my head, using a chopstick as a cigarette holder, pretending I was Jackie Brel, Jacques's long-lost but just as world-weary Mennonite twin. I couldn't believe that I was stuck in a town like Steinbach, where dancing was a sin and serving beer a felony.

There were other things I became aware of as well. That my grandmother was a vanilla alcoholic who believed she was a teetotaller. That seventy-five-year-old women who had borne thirteen children weren't allowed to speak to the church congregation, but that fifteen-year-old boys were. That every family had a secret. And I learned that my dad had been depressed all his life.

---

1 *Jacques Brel* Belgian singer-songwriter (1929–78) who became famous performing his poetic ballads in Paris clubs; *tam* Scottish soft hat similar to a beret.

I had wondered, when I was a kid, why he spent so much of the weekend in bed and why he didn't talk much at home. Occasionally he'd tell me, sometimes in tears, that he loved me very much and that he wished he were a better father, that he were more involved in my life. But I never felt the need for an apology. It made me happy and a bit envious to know that my dad's students were able to witness his humour and intelligence firsthand, to hear him expound on his favourite subjects: Canadian history, Canadian politics and Canadian newspapers. I remember watching him at work and marvelling at his energy and enthusiasm. I thought he looked very handsome when he rolled up his sleeves and tucked his tie in between the buttons of his shirt, his hands on his hips, all ready for business and hard work.

Teaching school—helping others make sense of the world—was a good profession for a man who was continuously struggling to find meaning in life. I think he needed his students as much as they needed him. By fulfilling his duties, he was also shoring up a psyche at risk of erosion.

Four years before his death he was forced to retire from teaching because of a heart attack and some small strokes. He managed to finish the book he was writing on Canada's prime ministers, but then he seemed to fade away. He spent more and more of his time in bed, in the dark, not getting up even to eat or wash, not interested in watching TV or listening to the radio. Despite our pleading and cajoling, despite the medication and visits to various doctors' offices, appointments he dutifully kept, and despite my mother's unwavering love, we felt we were losing him.

I know about brain chemistry and depression, but there's still a part of me that blames my dad's death on being Mennonite and living in that freaky, austere place where this world isn't good enough and admission into the next one, the perfect one, means everything, where every word and deed gets you closer to or farther away from eternal life. If you don't believe that then nothing Steinbach stands for will make sense. And if life doesn't make sense you lose yourself in it, your spirit decays. That's what I believed had happened to my dad, and that's why I hated my town.

In the weeks and months after his death, my mom and my sister and I tried to piece things together. William Ashdown, the executive director of the Mood Disorders Association of Manitoba, told us the number of mentally ill Mennonites is abnormally high. "We don't know if it's genetic or cultural," he said, "but the Steinbach area is one that we're vitally concerned about."

"It's the way the church delivers the message," says a Mennonite friend of mine, "the message of sin and accountability. To be human, basically, is to be a sinner. So a person, a real believer, starts to get down on himself, and where does it end? They say self-loathing is the cornerstone of depression, right?"

Years ago, the Mennonite Church practised something called "shunning," whereby if you were to leave your husband, or marry outside the Church, or elope, or drink, or in some way contravene the Church's laws or act "out of faith," you could be expelled from the Church and ignored, shunned by the entire community, including your own family. Depression or despair, as it would have been referred to then, was considered to be the result of a lack of faith and therefore could be another reason for shunning.

These days most Mennonites don't officially practise shunning, although William Ashdown claims there are still Mennonites from extreme conservative sects who are being shunned and shamed into silence within their communities for being mentally ill. Certainly Arden Thiessen, the minister of my dad's church, and a long-time friend of his, is aware of the causes of depression and the pain experienced by those who suffer from it. He doesn't see it as a lack of faith, but as an awful sickness.

But I can't help thinking that that history had just a little to do with my alcoholic grandmother's insisting that she was a non-drinker, and my dad's telling his doctors, smiling that beautiful smile of his, that he was fine, just fine.

Not long before he died my dad told me about the time he was five and was having his tonsils out. Just before the operation began he was knocked out with ether and he had a dream that he was somersaulting through the hospital walls, right through, easily, he said, moving his hands in circles through the air. It was wonderful. He told me he would never forget that feeling.

But mostly, the world was a sad and unsafe place for him, and his town provided shelter from it. Maybe he saw this as a gift, while I came to see it as oppression. He could peel back the layers of hypocrisy and intolerance and see what was good, and I couldn't. He believed that it mattered what he did in life, and he believed in the next world, one that's better. He kept the faith of his Mennonite forebears to the very end, or what he might call the beginning, and removed himself from this world entirely.

Stephanie, the waitress in the café in Woodridge, told my mother that my dad was calm and polite when he spoke to her, as if he were about to sit down to a cup of tea. She told her that he hadn't seemed at all afraid. But why would you be if you believed you were going to a place where there is no more sadness?

My dad never talked to us about God or religion. We didn't have family devotion like everybody else. He never quoted out loud from the Bible or lectured us about not going to church. In fact his only two pieces of advice to me were "Be yourself" and "You can do anything."

But he still went to church. It didn't matter how low he felt, or how cold it was outside. He would put on his suit and tie and stylish cap and walk the seven or eight blocks to church. He always walked, through searing heat or sub-arctic chill. If he was away on holidays he would find a church and go to it. At the lake he drove forty miles down gravel roads to attend an outdoor church in the bush. I think he needed church like a junkie needs a fix: to get him through another day in a world of pain.

What I love about my town is that it gave my dad the faith that stopped him from being afraid in those last violent seconds he spent on earth. And the place in my mind where we meet is on the front steps of my dad's church, the big one on Main Street across from Don's Bakery and the Goodwill store. We smile and talk for a few minutes outside, basking in the warmth of the summer sun he loved so much. Then he goes in and I stay outside, and we're both happy where we are.

—1999

Ivan Coyote
b. 1969

Ivan Coyote is a storyteller, performer, filmmaker, and author of more than ten books of fiction, non-fiction, and poetry. They[1] are a popular public speaker and an occasional commentator on transgender issues, including a widely viewed TED Talk on the need for gender-neutral bathrooms. Constantly on the road as a storyteller, entertainer, and public speaker, Coyote does not separate performance from writing, finding that the two are closely related: "Live performance has become the backbone of my editing process."

Coyote, whose gender is non-binary, is a self-proclaimed "gender failure," a phrase also used as the title of a collaborative show and book they created with the singer and writer Rae Spoon. Coyote's work has been praised for its portrayal of trans experience, as well as its "quietly radical" refusal "to centre trans-ness as the single primary concern in trans lives." They have also expressed frustration at the treatment of their work as a form of education or activism: "What would I be free to write and talk about if I wasn't always expected to change the world? What if I was just allowed to live and create in it?"

Coyote's writing, which includes memoir as well as fiction, is often inspired by their working-class upbringing in Whitehorse and, in their teenage years, Vancouver Island. Their Irish Catholic extended family also influenced the style of what Coyote calls their "kitchen table stories," intimate and funny narratives with roots in oral storytelling. The resulting work combines a down-to-earth tone with artistic sophistication: as one reviewer commented, "Coyote is poetic in their phrasing and plain spoken with their truths." Coyote's novel *Bow Grip* won the 2007 ReLit Award, and their short story collection *Close to Spider Man* was a finalist for the Danuta Gleed Award for Short Fiction.

Tomboys Still

Linda Gould was a friend of my mom's. Linda was from somewhere not here, somewhere not the Yukon, she had family down south and she had raven black hair. One time I asked my mom why Linda's name was Linda Gould but her husband was still called Don Dixon. My mom told me that some women chose not to take their husband's last name when they got married. It was 1974 and this impressed me for reasons I did not fully comprehend just yet.

Linda and Don lived in a rented house next to the clay cliffs downtown, and had one wall in their living room covered in that mural type of wallpaper,

---

1   Coyote's pronouns are they/them.

depicting a picture of a forest of giant pine trees. Linda wouldn't let Don paint over that wallpaper or tear it down; she said it reminded her of California.

I was a Yukon kid and had never seen a real tree that big in my life, I could only imagine them.

Linda played hockey, and she also coached a girl's ringette team. As soon as I turned five years old I was allowed to join up. I had never really heard of the game called ringette but wanted to be good at it because Linda was good at it. It turned out ringette was kind of like hockey light, but only girls played it. It wasn't as much fun as hockey looked like it was, but I kept going to practices because my mom had spent all that money on skates and a helmet for me. There were barely enough girls to make one team so we never got to play a real game, we mostly skated around and practiced stopping. That's the truth, and also a metaphor. Some of the girls came in figure skates, but not me.

One day Don Dixon showed up early at practice and watched us run a passing drill for a while. He told Linda after practice that I was already a better skater than half the boys on the Squirts team he coached and so did I want to come and play with the boys? he asked.

I didn't even have to think before I said yes. My mom said hold on, she had to talk it over with my dad, who was only half listening because he was reading that book *Shogun*[1] and it was a super good book he said, and my mom said yes, I guess, you can play hockey, but be careful out there. Linda taught me how to do a slap shot and told me never to skate with my head down. I was the only girl playing in the Whitehorse Minor Hockey League for eleven years after that. I made it all the way up to junior hockey. Left wing.

When I turned sixteen they wouldn't let me play hockey with the boys anymore. I was now a legal liability, they told my parents, and the minor hockey league just couldn't afford that kind of insurance, and besides, what if I got hurt, the boys were so much bigger now, plus body-checking. Come and play on the women's team with us, Linda said, and so I did.

That was how I met Donna Doucette, who played defence and worked as a bartender at the Kopper King on the Alaska Highway. Donna Doucette wore her long brown hair in a whip-like braid that swung between her shoulder blades when she skated back hard for the puck. I think I pretty much fell in love with Donna Doucette the first time I saw her spit perfectly through the square holes in the face mask on her helmet. She just curled her tongue into a tube and horked unapologetically right through her mask. It shot like a bullet, about fifteen feet, straight out onto the ice. I had never seen a woman do anything like that before, I could only imagine the back-of-the-head slap

---

1   *Shogun* 1975 novel by James Clavell.

my gran would lay on me if I ever dared to spit anywhere in public, much less turn it into an art form like Donna Doucette did.

I remember hearing her playing fastball one midnight sunny summer evening; I was playing softball on the field next to the women's league. All the women on my hockey team played ball together in the summer; like serious fast pitch, they were not fooling around. Hockey was for sport but fast pitch was for keeps. Donna Doucette played shortstop and would spare no skin to make a catch, and she spat all over the goddamn place out there on the field too, and cussed and catcalled. Hey batter batta batta swing batta batta. I remember her in silhouette, bobbing back and forth on the toes of her cleats, all backlit by the sun and gum a-chew, a mouthy shadow, punching the pocket of her gloved hand with her red-nailed fingertips coiled into a fist.

That's the thing about Linda and Donna. They weren't like me. Linda wore sapphire studs in her ears and a red red dress to our Christmas party. Donna swore and stole third base wearing what my mother claimed to be too much eye makeup for daylight hours, which even back then I thought was kind of harsh, it being summer in the Yukon and it never really getting dark and all.

Donna and Linda. My memories of them are sharp, hyper-focused. I was paying attention to every detail of them, I was searching them for clues to who I wanted to be, but I already knew I couldn't be like them. I wanted something else. Something close to what they had. They hinted at a kind of freedom, a kind of just not giving a fuck what anyone said about them that made me want things I didn't know the words for.

Theresa Turner drove her two-stroke dirt bike to school every day we were in grade eleven, appearing out of the willows and trailing a tail of dust as she gunned the throttle and skidded to a stop by the tree line at the edge of our high school parking lot. She would dismount and stomp her kickstand down with the heel of her buckled biker boot and shake her mane of mahogany ringlets loose from under her helmet and strut in her skin-tight Levi 501s past the heads smoking cigarettes by the back double doors to the wood shop. Fuck you looking at? she would sneer at them. This for some reason made them blush, and pretend they weren't watching her ass swing as the door hissed shut behind her. I was old enough by then to be full-on smitten.

Carolyn O'Hara was Theresa Turner's very best friend from Cedar. Cedar was a suburb of the pulp mill town of Nanaimo where I was living with my grandmother. Theresa Turner and Carolyn O'Hara had grown up out there together and had known each other all their lives. They also knew all about all the boys from the rural working class outskirts of Nanaimo. Knew all the boys who had to skip school in the fall to bring in the hay and miss entire weeks in the spring when the lambs came.

They knew all about the boys with the jean jacket vests with ZZ Top or Judas Priest[1] album covers recreated in ballpoint ink. Houses of the Holy.[2] The boys whose older brothers were doing time.

Carolyn O'Hara had a necklace strung of these diamonds in the rough, these boys who would punch locker doors and prick the skin in between their forefinger and thumb and rub ink into it in the shape of a broken heart all for the love of Carolyn O'Hara. She had her brother who died in a motorcycle accident's acoustic guitar and she would play "Walk on the Wild Side" by Lou Reed at lunch. I remember her swinging her honey-brown hair in the sun in the front seat of Eddie Bartolo's midnight blue Nova with the windows rolled down and saying, "So what if I am on the rag, you asshole. I'd like to see you go to gym class and do your fucking flexed arm hang exercises if you'd been bleeding out of your ass like it's going out of goddamn style for the last three fucking days. You going to smoke that thing or pass it on, you selfish bastard?"

Carolyn O'Hara could out-swear even Theresa Turner, it's why they were the perfect pair. Carolyn O'Hara was gorgeous. Could have been a model, everybody said so, but she was very practical and took the dental hygienist's program up at the college right after we graduated.

I ran into Theresa one day about five years ago, on my way to Vancouver Island for a gig. Theresa was wearing false eyelashes and an orange reflective vest at the same time, which I thought was awesome. Hugged me hard and told me she had been working for BC Ferries for seventeen years now, doing what my gran had always said was a good, clean, union job if you liked people. Said Carolyn O'Hara had opened her own dog grooming business. A real cool place where you can drop your dog off to get groomed, or rent a big tub and wash your own dog in the back. She said they were both happy, they still kept in real good touch, in fact they were going for mani-pedis for their fortieth birthdays just next week.

Mia Telerico. Fall of 1992, she had just moved to town from Toronto. I met her in my friend's coffee shop on the Drive, she smoked Du Maurier Light King Size and I smoked Player's Light regulars. I, for reasons unexamined by me at the time, I guess I was trying to impress her, so I spontaneously leapt up and did a dramatic reading for her of *The Cat in the Hat*, and we briefly became lovers, and then, so far, life-long friends. Mia Telerico said in my kitchen one night that first winter It's E-Talian, not Eye-Talian, you sound like a redneck if you say it wrong, and then she showed me how to peel a bunch of garlic all at once by crushing it with the side of the butcher knife.

---

1   *ZZ Top ... Judas Priest* Bands that became popular in the early 1970s.
2   *Houses of the Holy* 1973 album by Led Zeppelin.

How many ways do I love Mia Telerico? I love that she refinishes furniture and owns all her own power tools and that it takes hours for her curls to dry so she has special hair-washing days, because washing her hair is like, a thing, right, and she is missing part of a finger from an accident she had cleaning the chain on her motorcycle and she is tough as nails but with the softest heart and bosom, can I even use the word "bosom" anymore? I don't know. Her hugs feel better than nearly anything is all I'm saying, and when she lets me rest my head there for a second I feel so untouchable, so unhurtable somehow, so magically protected by her soft cheek and rough hands ever capable. I called her just now and left a message asking her if it was okay if I called her a femme tomboy, how does she feel about me pinning those words on her femme tomboy, but really, all I'm trying to do here is broaden the joining, I tell her voice mail. All I want to do is honour all the femme tomboys I have ever loved, and thank them for showing me the possibilities. Anyway. Mia's father was from Malta and her mother is Italian and her dad was a janitor and her ma worked in a chocolate factory just like I Love Lucy and Ethel[1] except less funny and for decades until it wrecked her back.

I left Mia Telerico a message but I haven't heard back yet. I hear through the grapevine that she is going through a breakup and, well, I guess I am too, and both of us, we take these things pretty hard, artist's hearts pumping just beneath the skin of our chests like they do.

—2016

---

1   *I Love Lucy and Ethel* Reference to a popular episode of the *I Love Lucy* sitcom (1951–57), in which Lucy and Ethel struggle to keep up with the assembly line in a chocolate factory.

Glossary

Aesthetes: members of a late nineteenth-century movement that valued "art for art's sake"—for its purely aesthetic qualities, as opposed to valuing art for the moral content it may convey, for the intellectual stimulation it may provide, or for a range of other qualities.

Allegory: a narrative with both a literal meaning and secondary, often symbolic meaning or meanings. Allegory frequently employs personification to give concrete embodiment to abstract concepts or entities, such as feelings or personal qualities. It may also present one set of characters or events in the guise of another, using implied parallels for the purposes of satire or political comment.

Alliteration: the grouping of words with the same initial consonant (e.g., "break, blow, burn, and make me new"). See also *assonance*.

Allusion: a reference, often indirect or unidentified, to a person, thing, or event. A reference in one literary work to another literary work, whether to its content or its form, also constitutes an allusion.

Ambiguity: an "opening" of language created by the writer to allow for multiple meanings or differing interpretations. In literature, ambiguity may be deliberately employed by the writer to enrich meaning; this differs from any unintentional, unwanted ambiguity in non-literary prose.

Anachronism: accidentally or intentionally attributing people, things, ideas, and events to historical periods in which they do not and could not possibly belong.

Analepsis: see *flashback*.

Analogy: a broad term that refers to our processes of noting similarities among things or events. Specific forms of analogy include *simile* and *metaphor*.

Apostrophe: a figure of speech (a *trope*; see *figures of speech*) in which a writer directly addresses an object—or a dead or absent person—as if the imagined audience were actually listening.

Archetype: in literature and mythology, a recurring idea, symbol, motif, character, or place. To some scholars and psychologists, an archetype represents universal human thought-patterns or experiences.

Assonance: the repetition of identical or similar vowel sounds in stressed syllables in which the surrounding consonants are different: for example, "shame" and "fate"; "gale" and "cage"; or the long "i" sounds in "Beside the pumice isle...."

Atmosphere: see *tone*.

Baroque: powerful and heavily ornamented in style. "Baroque" is a term from the history of visual art and of music that is sometimes also used to describe certain literary styles.

Bathos: an anticlimactic effect brought about by a writer's descent from an elevated subject or tone to the ordinary or trivial.

Black Comedy: humour based on death, horror, or any incongruously macabre subject matter.

Bombast: inappropriately inflated or grandiose language.

Burlesque: satire of an exaggerated sort, particularly that which ridicules its subject by emphasizing its vulgar or ridiculous aspects.

Canon: in literature, those works that are commonly accepted as possessing authority or importance. In practice, "canonical" texts or authors are those that are discussed most frequently by scholars and taught most frequently in university courses.

Caricature: an exaggerated and simplified depiction of character; the reduction of a personality to one or two telling traits at the expense of all other nuances and contradictions.

Carpe Diem: Latin (from Horace) meaning "seize the day." The idea of enjoying the moment is a common one in Renaissance love poetry.

Characterization: the means by which an author develops and presents a character's personality qualities and distinguishing traits. A character may be established in the story by descriptive commentary or may be developed less directly—for example, through his or her words, actions, thoughts, and interactions with other characters.

Chronology: the way a story is organized in terms of time. Linear narratives run continuously from one point in time to a later point, while non-linear narratives are non-continuous and may jump forward and backward in time. A *flashback*, in which a story jumps to a scene previous in time, is an example of non-linearity.

Classical: originating in or relating to ancient Greek or Roman culture. As commonly conceived, *classical* implies a strong sense of formal order. The term *neoclassical* is often used with reference to literature of the Restoration and eighteenth century that was strongly influenced by ancient Greek and Roman models.

Comedy: as a literary term, used originally to denote that class of ancient Greek drama in which the action ends happily. More broadly the term has been used to describe a wide variety of literary forms of a more or less light-hearted character.

Conceit: an unusually elaborate metaphor or simile that extends beyond its original tenor and vehicle, sometimes becoming a "master" analogy for the entire work (see, for example, Donne's "The Flea"). Ingenious or fanciful images and comparisons were especially popular with the metaphysical poets of the seventeenth century, giving rise to the term "metaphysical conceit."

Conflict: struggles between characters and opposing forces. Conflict can be internal (psychological) or external (conflict with another character, for instance, or with society or nature).

Connotation: the implied, often unspoken meaning(s) of a given word, as distinct from its *denotation*, or literal meaning. Connotations may have highly emotional undertones and are usually culturally specific.

Convention: aesthetic approach, technique, or practice accepted as characteristic and appropriate for a particular form. It is a convention of certain sorts of plays, for example, that the characters speak in blank verse, of other sorts of plays that characters speak in rhymed couplets, and of still other sorts of dramatic performances that characters frequently break into song to express their feelings.

Denotation: see *connotation*.

Dénouement: that portion of a narrative that follows a dramatic climax, in which conflicts are resolved and the narrative is brought to a close. Traditional accounts of narrative structure often posit a triangle or arc, with rising action followed by a climax and then by a dénouement. (Such accounts bear little relation, however, to the ways in which most actual narratives are structured—particularly most twentieth- and twenty-first-century literary fictions.)

Dialogue: words spoken by characters to one another. (When a character is addressing him or her self or the audience directly, the words spoken are referred to as a *soliloquy*.)

Diction: word choice. Whether the diction of a literary work (or of a literary character) is colloquial, conversational, formal, or of some other type contributes significantly to the tone of the text as well as to characterization.

Didacticism: aesthetic approach emphasizing moral instruction.

Dramatic Irony: this form of *irony* occurs when an audience has access to information not available to the character.

Ellipsis: the omission of a word or words necessary for the complete grammatical construction of a sentence, but not necessary for our understanding of the sentence.

Epigraph: a quotation placed at the beginning of a work to indicate or foreshadow the theme.

Epiphany: a moment at which matters of significance are suddenly illuminated for a literary character (or for the reader), typically triggered by something small and seemingly of little import. The term first came into wide currency in connection with the fiction of James Joyce.

Ethos: the perceived character, trustworthiness, or credibility of a writer or narrator.

Euphemism: mode of expression through which aspects of reality considered to be vulgar, crudely physical, or unpleasant are referred to indirectly rather than named explicitly. A variety of euphemisms exist for the processes of urination and defecation; *passed away* is often used as a euphemism for *died.*

Euphony: pleasant, musical sounds or rhythms.

Existentialism: a philosophical approach according to which the meaning of human life is derived from the actual experience of the living individual. The existential worldview, in which life is assumed to have no essential or pre-existing meanings other than those we personally choose to endow it with, can produce an absurdist sensibility.

Exposition: the setting out of material in an ordered (and usually concise) form, either in speech or in writing. In a play those parts of the action that do not occur on stage but are rather recounted by the characters are frequently described as being presented in exposition. Similarly, when the background narrative is filled in near the beginning of a novel, such material is often described as having been presented in exposition.

Farce: sometimes classed as the "lowest" form of *comedy*. Its humour depends not on verbal wit, but on physicality and sight gags.

Fiction: imagined or invented narrative. In literature, the term is usually used to refer to prose narratives (such as novels and short stories).

Figures of Speech: deliberate, highly concentrated uses of language to achieve particular purposes or effects on an audience. There are two kinds of figures: schemes and *tropes*. Schemes involve changes in word-sound and word-order, such as *alliteration*. Tropes play on our understandings of words to extend, alter, or transform meaning, as in *metaphor* and *personification.*

First-Person Narrative: narrative recounted using *I* and *me*. See also *narrative perspective.*

Flashback: in fiction, the inclusion in the primary thread of a story's narrative of a scene (or scenes) from an earlier point in time. Flashbacks may be used to revisit from a different viewpoint events that have already been recounted in the main thread of narrative; to present material that has been left out in the initial recounting; or to present relevant material from a time before the beginning of the main thread of narrative. The use of flashbacks in fiction is sometimes referred to as *analepsis*.

Flashforward: the inclusion in the primary thread of a story's narrative of a scene (or scenes) from a later point in time.

Flat Character: the opposite of a round character, a flat character is defined by a small number of traits and does not possess enough complexity to be psychologically realistic. "Flat character" can be a disparaging term, but need not be; flat characters serve different purposes in a fiction than round characters, and are often better suited to some types of literature, such as allegory or farcical comedy.

Foil: in literature, a character whose behaviour and/or qualities set in relief for the reader or audience those of a strongly contrasting character who plays a more central part in the story.

Genre: a class or type of literary work. The concept of genre may be used with different levels of generality. At the most general, poetry, drama, and prose fiction are distinguished as separate genres. At a lower level of generality various sub-genres are frequently distinguished, such as (within the genre of prose fiction) the novel, the novella, and the short story; and, at a still lower level of generality, the mystery novel, the detective novel, the novel of manners, and so on.

Gothic: in architecture and the visual arts, a term used to describe styles prevalent from the twelfth to the fourteenth centuries, but in literature a term used to describe work with a sinister or grotesque tone that seeks to evoke a sense of terror on the part of the reader or audience. Gothic literature originated as a genre in the eighteenth century with works such as Horace Walpole's *The Castle of Otranto*. To some extent the notion of the medieval itself then carried with it associations of the dark and the grotesque, but from the beginning an element of intentional exaggeration (sometimes verging on self-parody) attached itself to the genre. The Gothic trend of youth culture that began in the late twentieth century is less clearly associated with the medieval, but shares with the various varieties of Gothic literature (from Walpole in the eighteenth century, to Bram Stoker in the early twentieth, to Stephen King and Anne Rice in the late twentieth) a fondness for the sensational and the grotesque, as well as a propensity to self-parody.

Grotesque: literature of the grotesque is characterized by a focus on extreme or distorted aspects of human characteristics. (The term can also refer particularly to a character who is odd or disturbing.) This focus can serve to comment on and challenge societal norms.

Hyperbole: a *figure of speech* (a *trope*) that deliberately exaggerates or inflates meaning to achieve particular effects, such as the irony in A.E. Housman's claim (from "Terence, This Is Stupid Stuff") that "malt does more than Milton can / To justify God's ways to man."

Image: a representation of a sensory experience or of an object that can be known by the senses.

Imagery: the range of images in a given work. We can gain much insight into works by looking for patterns of imagery. For example, the imagery of spring (budding trees, rain, singing birds) in Kate Chopin's "The Story of an Hour" reinforces the suggestions of death and rebirth in the plot and theme.

Incantation: a chant or recitation of words that are believed to have magical power. A poem can achieve an "incantatory" effect through a compelling rhyme scheme and other repetitive patterns.

Intertextuality: the act of bringing one cultural text into relationship with another, as when a writer references a painting, a song title or lyric, another novel, poem, or play, a famous theoretical work, etc. A literary text may connect with other cultural texts via *allusion*, *parody*, or *satire*, or in a variety of other ways.

Irony: the use of irony draws attention to a gap between what is said and what is meant, or what appears to be true and what is true. Types of irony include verbal irony (which includes *hyberbole*, *litotes*, and *sarcasm*), *dramatic irony*, and structural irony (in which the gap between what is "said" and meant is sustained throughout an entire piece, as when an author makes use of an unreliable narrator or speaker).

Litotes: a *figure of speech* (a *trope*) in which a writer deliberately uses understatement to highlight the importance of an argument, or to convey an ironic attitude.

Metaphor: a *figure of speech* (in this case, a *trope*) in which a comparison is made or identity is asserted between two unrelated things or actions without the use of "like" or "as."

Metonymy: a *figure of speech* (a *trope*), meaning "change of name," in which a writer refers to an object or idea by substituting the name of another object or idea closely associated with it: for example, the substitution of "crown" for monarchy, "the press" for journalism, or "the pen" for writing. *Synecdoche* is a kind of metonymy.

Modernism: in the history of literature, music, and the visual arts, a movement that began in the early twentieth century, characterized by a thoroughgoing rejection of the then-dominant conventions of literary plotting and characterization, of melody and harmony, and of perspective and other naturalistic forms of visual representation. In literature (as in music and the visual arts), modernists endeavoured to represent the complexity of what seemed to them to be an increasingly fragmented world by adopting techniques of presenting story material, illuminating character, and employing imagery that emphasized (in the words of Virginia Woolf) "the spasmodic, the obscure, the fragmentary."

Mood: this can describe the writer's attitude, implied or expressed, toward the subject (see *tone*); or it may refer to the atmosphere that a writer creates in a passage of description or narration.

Motif: pattern formed by the recurrence of an idea, image, action, or plot element throughout a literary work, creating new levels of meaning and strengthening structural coherence. The term is taken from music, where it describes recurring melodies or themes. See also *theme*.

Motivation: the forces that seem to cause characters to act, or reasons why characters do what they do.

Narration: the process of disclosing information, whether fictional or non-fictional.

Narrative Perspective: in fiction, the point of view from which a story is narrated. A first-person narrative is recounted using *I* and *me*, whereas a third-person narrative is recounted using *he, she, they*, and so on. When a narrative is written in the third person and the narrative voice evidently "knows" all that is being done and thought, the story is typically described as being recounted by an "omniscient narrator." Second-person narratives, in which the narrative is recounted using *you*, are very rare.

Narrator: the voice (or voices) disclosing information. In fiction, the narrator is distinguished from both the author (a real, historical person) and the implied author (whom the reader imagines the author to be). Narrators can also be distinguished according to the degree to which they share the reality of the other characters in the story and the extent to which they participate in the action; according to how much information they are privy to (and how much of that information they are willing to share with the reader); and according to whether or not they are perceived by the reader as reliable or unreliable sources of information. See also *narrative perspective*.

Neoclassicism: literally the "new classicism," the aesthetic style that dominated high culture in Europe through the seventeenth and eighteenth centuries, and in some places into the nineteenth century. Its subject matter was often taken from Greek and Roman myth and history; in *style*, it valued order, reason, clarity, and moderation.

Onomatopoeia: a *figure of speech* (a scheme) in which a word "imitates" a sound, or in which the sound of a word seems to reflect its meaning.

Oxymoron: a *figure of speech* (a *trope*) in which two words whose meanings seem contradictory are placed together; we see an example in Shakespeare's *Twelfth Night*, when Orsino refers to the "sweet pangs" of love.

Parable: a story told to illustrate a moral principle. It differs from *allegory* in being shorter and simpler: parables do not generally function on two levels simultaneously.

Parody: a close, usually mocking imitation of a particular literary work, or of the well-known style of a particular author, in order to expose or magnify weaknesses. Parody is a form of *satire*—that is, humour that may ridicule and scorn its object.

Pastiche: a discourse that borrows or imitates other writers' characters, forms, style, or ideas, sometimes creating something of a literary patchwork. Unlike a parody, a pastiche can be intended as a compliment to the original writer.

Pathetic Fallacy: a form of *personification* in which inanimate objects are given human emotions: for example, rain clouds "weeping." The word "fallacy" in this connection is intended to suggest the distortion of reality or the false emotion that may result from an exaggerated use of personification.

Pathos: the emotional quality of a discourse; or the ability of a discourse to appeal to our emotions. It is usually applied to the mood conveyed by images of pain, suffering, or loss that arouse feelings of pity or sorrow in the reader.

Persona: the assumed identity or "speaking voice" that a writer projects in a discourse. The term "persona" literally means "mask."

Personification: a *figure of speech* (a *trope*), also known as "prosopopoeia," in which a writer refers to inanimate objects, ideas, or non-human animals as if they were human, or creates a human figure to represent an abstract entity such as Philosophy or Peace.

Phoneme: a linguistic term denoting the smallest unit of sound that it is possible to distinguish. The words *fun* and *phone* each have three phonemes, though one has three letters and one has five.

Point of View: see *narrative perspective*.

Postmodernism: in literature and the visual arts, a movement influential in the late twentieth and early twenty-first centuries. In some ways postmodernism represents a reaction to modernism, in others an extension of it. With roots in the work of French philosophers such as Jacques Derrida and Michel Foucault, it is deeply coloured by theory; indeed, it may be said to have begun at the "meta" level of theorizing rather than at the level of practice. Like modernism, postmodernism embraces difficulty and distrusts the simple and straightforward. More broadly, postmodernism is characterized by a rejection of absolute truth or value, of closed systems, of grand unified narratives.

Postmodernist fiction is characterized by a frequently ironic or playful tone in dealing with reality and illusion; by a willingness to combine different styles or forms in a single work (just as in architecture the postmodernist spirit embodies a willingness to borrow from seemingly disparate styles in designing a single structure); and by a highly attuned awareness of the problematized state of the writer, artist, or theorist as observer.

Protagonist: the central character in a literary work.

Pun: a play on words, in which a word with two or more distinct meanings, or two words with similar sounds, may create humorous ambiguities. Also known as "paranomasia."

Realism: as a literary term, the presentation through literature of material closely resembling real life. As notions both of what constitutes "real life" and of how it may be most faithfully represented in literature have varied widely, "realism" has taken a variety of meanings. The term "naturalistic" has sometimes been used as a synonym for *realistic*; naturalism originated in the nineteenth century as a term denoting a form of realism focusing in particular on grim, unpleasant, or ugly aspects of the real.

Rhetoric: in classical Greece and Rome, the art of persuasion and public speaking. From the Middle Ages onwards, the study of rhetoric gave greater attention to style, particularly *figures of speech*. Today in poetics, the term rhetoric may encompass not only figures of speech, but also the persuasive effects of forms, sounds, and word choices.

Romance: a dreamlike genre of fiction or storytelling in which the ordinary laws of nature are suspended—in which, for example, statues come to life, or shipwrecked men emerge from the sea unharmed.

Romanticism: a major social and cultural movement, originating in Europe, that shaped much of Western artistic thought in the late eighteenth and nineteenth centuries. Opposing the ideal of controlled, rational order associated with the Enlightenment, Romanticism emphasizes the importance of spontaneous self-expression, emotion, and personal experience in producing art. In Romanticism, the "natural" is privileged over the conventional or the artificial.

Sarcasm: a form of *irony* (usually spoken) in which the meaning is conveyed largely by the tone of voice adopted; something said sarcastically is meant to imply its opposite.

Satire: literary work designed to make fun of or seriously criticize its subject. According to many literary theories of the Renaissance and neoclassical periods, the ridicule through satire of a certain sort of behaviour may function for the reader or audience as a corrective of such behaviour.

Setting: the time, place, and cultural environment in which a story or work takes place.

Simile: a *figure of speech* (a *trope*) which makes an explicit comparison between a particular object and another object or idea that is similar in some (often unexpected) way. A simile always uses "like" or "as" to signal the connection. Compare with *metaphor*.

Style: a distinctive or specific use of language and form.

Sublime: a concept, popular in eighteenth-century England, that sought to capture the qualities of grandeur, power, and awe that may be inherent in or produced by undomesticated nature or great art. The sublime was thought of as higher and loftier than something that is merely beautiful.

Subtext: implied or suggested meaning of a passage of text, or of an entire work.

Surrealism: Surrealism incorporates elements of the true appearance of life and nature, combining these elements according to a logic more typical of dreams than waking life. Isolated aspects of surrealist art may create powerful illusions of reality, but the effect of the whole is usually to disturb or question our sense of reality rather than to confirm it.

Syllable: vocal sound or group of sounds forming a unit of speech; a syllable may be formed with a single effort of articulation. Some syllables consist of a single phoneme (e.g., the word *I*, or the first syllable in the word *u*-ni-ty) but others may be made up of several phonemes (as with one-syllable words such as *lengths, splurged,* and *through*). By contrast, the much shorter words *ago, any,* and *open* each have two syllables.

Symbol: something that represents itself but goes beyond this in suggesting other meanings. Like metaphor, the symbol extends meaning; but while the tenor and vehicle of metaphor are bound in a specific relationship, a symbol may have a range of connotations. For example, the image of a rose may call forth associations of love, passion, transience, fragility, youth, and beauty, among others. Depending upon the context, such an image could be interpreted in a variety of ways.

Synecdoche: a kind of *metonymy* in which a writer substitutes the name of a part of something to signify the whole: for example, "sail" for ship or "hand" for a member of the ship's crew.

Syntax: the ordering of words in a sentence.

Theme: in general, an idea explored in a work through character, action, and/or image. To be fully developed, however, a theme must consist of more than a single concept or idea: it should also include an argument about the idea. Thus if a poem examines the topic of jealousy, we might say the theme is that jealousy undermines love or jealousy is a manifestation of insecurity. Few, if any, literary works have single themes.

Tone: the writer's attitude toward a given subject or audience, as expressed through an authorial persona or "voice." Tone can be projected through particular choices of wording, imagery, figures of speech, and rhythmic devices. Compare *mood*.

Tragedy: in the traditional definition originating in discussions of ancient Greek drama, a serious narrative recounting the downfall of the protagonist, usually a person of high social standing. More loosely, the term has been applied to a wide variety of literary forms in which the tone is predominantly a dark one and the narrative does not end happily.

Trope: any figure of speech that plays on our understandings of words to extend, alter, or transform "literal" meaning. Common tropes include *metaphor, simile, personification, hyperbole, metonymy, oxymoron, synecdoche,* and *irony.* See also *figures of speech.*

Acknowledgement: The glossary for *The Broadview Introduction to Literature* incorporates some material initially prepared for the following Broadview anthologies: *The Broadview Anthology of Poetry*, edited by Herbert Rosengarten and Amanda Goldrick-Jones; *The Broadview Anthology of Drama*, edited by Jennifer Wise and Craig Walker; *The Broadview Anthology of Short Fiction*, edited by Julia Gaunce et al.; *The Broadview Anthology of British Literature*, edited by Joseph Black et al. The editors gratefully acknowledge the contributions of the editors of these other anthologies. Please note that all material in the glossary, whether initially published in another Broadview anthology or appearing here for the first time, is protected by copyright.

Permissions Acknowledgements

Index of Authors and Titles

From the Publisher

A name never says it all, but the word "Broadview" expresses a good deal of the philosophy behind our company. We are open to a broad range of academic approaches and political viewpoints. We pay attention to the broad impact book publishing and book printing has in the wider world; we began using recycled stock more than a decade ago, and for some years now we have used 100% recycled paper for most titles. Our publishing program is internationally oriented and broad-ranging. Our individual titles often appeal to a broad readership too; many are of interest as much to general readers as to academics and students.

Founded in 1985, Broadview remains a fully independent company owned by its shareholders—not an imprint or subsidiary of a larger multinational.

For the most accurate information on our books (including information on pricing, editions, and formats) please visit our website at www.broadviewpress.com. Our print books and ebooks are also available for sale on our site.

broadview press

www.broadviewpress.com

This book is made of paper from well-managed FSC® - certified forests, recycled materials, and other controlled sources.